WHEN WE LISTEN

Recognizing the Potential
of Urban Youth

SYLVESTER BROWN, JR. DIRECTOR OF THE SWEET POTATO PROJECT
FORWARD BY CHEF JEFF HENDERSON

Editor: Jourdan Lee

Cover and Book Design: Lacey O'Connor

Photography: Benjamin Gandhi-Shepard, Richard Reilly and Chuck Ramsey

Printed in the United States of America

First Printing, 2019

This book is dedicated to the students of the Sweet Potato Project (2012-2018)

ADVANCE PRAISE

Sylvester Brown is the real deal. He draws from real life experiences to help today's youth forge a promising future. A must read and a must share with a young person you know. —Maxine Clark / Founder, Build-A-Bear Workshop

Sylvester Brown sees the beauty, the brilliance, the curiosity, and the love of Black children. Do your soul a favor and read this book.—Walter Johnson, Author of *River of Dark Dreams: Slavery and Empire in the Mississippi Valley's Cotton Kingdom*

I predict that Learning to Listen will become a valuable addition to anyone's library. For me, it serves as a model for uplifting young people. It's an in-your-face testament to what they deal with while growing up poor. —Chef Jeff Henderson, Author of *If You Can See it, You Can Be it*

As an educator, I know what happens when you unleash the potential of young people – they catch fire, they grow. Please read this book. Help change the lives of our youth. If you do, they will immediately change the world.—Brad Stock, Distinguished Professor, Dept. of Religion and Philosophy, Principia College

Sylvester Brown's book, *When We Listen* encourages us to hear the messages of "Old"; do for self, do it for the children. Out of the mouths of children, a child shall lead.—Robert A. Powell, Founder and Executive Director Portfolio Gallery and Educational Center

CONTENTS

FORWARD

By Chef Jeff Henderson

It's always a pleasure meeting like-minded people. It's a special treat when they're, like me, products of the 'hood, trying in some way, large or small, to give back to young people raised in trying conditions like they had growing up.

Sylvester Brown, Jr. is one such brother. We met in 2012, months before he started his Sweet Potato Project. As a gifted writer, my publishers recommended Sylvester as a consultant and researcher for my critically-acclaimed book, *If You Can See It, You Can Be It.*

As a potential collaborator, I wanted Sylvester to get to know the real me. I wanted him to not only know my story as a successful chef, public speaker and author but to understand my true passion: talking, motivating and working with at-risk youth in the darkest environments on earth—juvenile detention centers or prisons.

As I do in many of the cities I visit, I spent time with a group of youth at the St. Louis Juvenile Detention Center. Sylvester recounts that experience in this book, so I won't repeat it here. What I want to do, however, is talk about how, during that visit, he mentioned his desire to start a program that would teach inner-city youth how to become entrepreneurs through growing food on vacant, abandoned lots and turning produce into products that they could sell.

I was immediately hooked by the potential of his concept. It tapped into my childhood memories before entering the drug game during the 1980s. You see, I was born with that entrepreneurial gene, too. As a youngster, I became the number one newspaper and candy-seller in my neighborhood. I discovered early that I had a gift of gab. I was that little homeboy knocking on stranger's doors asking to cut their grass before or after school. I was a "hustle-preneur" long before I coined the phrase.

I know from experience that there are young people, especially those who have inherited poverty, who have certain traits that can be nurtured, cultivated and flipped to become positive and productive aspects of life. But it's a strategic, purposeful, multi-faceted process.

When Sylvester talked about the Sweet Potato Project, I immediately recognized the long-term strategy and down-to-earth process that would allow him to tap into the hopes, dreams and ambitions of young people who have entrepreneurial potential but no idea what to do with it.

I was honored when he called to ask me to write the forward for this book. Once again, he had me within a few sentences. Honestly, I have been watching his project from afar. I've seen him as he's had teens plant seeds, harvest, make sweet potato products and become empowered through the power of food. We've talked on occasion about his challenges and struggles to raise money for the program, but he hasn't given up hope. His work, since leaving the *St. Louis Post-Dispatch* in 2009, has been solely devoted to economic development and rebuilding and revitalizing disadvantaged neighborhoods. As a brilliant researcher and writer, Sylvester has outlined the many challenges our youth face like poverty, incarceration, homelessness, trauma, low self-esteem, an inadequate educational system and a society that's more than anxious to lock up black, brown and poor white youth. This book serves as a template for anyone interested in helping disadvantaged youth be the best they can be.

Mostly, I meet with young people already locked up in the juvenile system. Sylvester's program and this book serve as preventive alternatives to incarcerating youth. His mission is to get them before they become criminalized. He wants to see more programs designed specifically to get troubled kids to use their natural, inherited traits not for the negative but the good.

What I like most about this book is its intention to help marginalized youth dream again. Sylvester and I understand that our young people are great observers of their worlds. Sometimes this intense analysis deters or alters their dreams. I remember as a kid, I had this great characteristic of studying people and environments. I remember pressing my face against the school bus window looking at nice, suburban homes. My young mind questioned why some people lived cozy, upper-to-middle-class lifestyles while the people around me lived in utter poverty. I understood the differences between the haves and the have nots early in life. Without direction or successful role models in my life, I became determined to "get mine" by any means necessary. Of course, that decision came with life-altering consequences.

In this book, Sylvester seeks to fill a role I never had in my youth.

He preaches about investing in the mental potential of low-income youth. We share the belief that these kids are brilliant, smart, innovative and full of possibilities. They're critical-thinkers and some are great communicators. They're waiting for someone to give them a platform to stand on and grow from.

When I was growing up, no one had conversations about college with me. Today, with poor black, brown and white families, expensive higher education is still not a realistic discussion at the dinner table. But, what's great about America is that it's full of opportunities. Sylvester's Sweet Potato Project program gives kids a right-now, right-here option for entrepreneurship. They don't have to be rocket scientists or even have college degrees to plant something in the ground and create a sellable product that people love to eat, that's great for the community, with great health benefits and has the added benefit of making money.

Sylvester knows that many youth, like those who've become part of his program, have never been exposed to opportunities outside their poor, deprived inner-city zones. Many wear the blinders of poverty that can blot available economic opportunities around them. Sylvester is creating avenues where our children can see, hear and experience love, validation, respect and mentorship—all the things upper and middle-class kids have implanted in their lives at early ages.

I know how valuable this book will be for those working with young people. As an advocate for youth who came from an impoverished inner-city community, I'm always trying to convince employers, educators and people in the corporate or juvenile justice system to invest in the natural resources and hidden talent of our inner-city kids.

This book reminds me that I must make a concerted effort to not just speak to youth but listen in return. If we look at their environments, hear their challenges and how they react to them, and truly listen to what young people are trying to tell us; we may stumble upon one of the key elements in saving their lives. There are certain inherited traits that come with being born in poverty. Young people know how to navigate and survive it. They know how to make a dollar out of 15 cents and create a meal out of crumbs and left-overs. Those survival instincts are developed early in their lives which, honestly, are key traits of any successful business person.

Young people have something to tell us and show us. At-risk kids were born on the edge. They live every day in survival mode and are taught not to complain. Unfortunately, they're also exposed to the wheelers & dealers, the movers & shakers in their communities— some involved in illegal activities. They hear and see street-level entrepreneurism, and some are drawn to the criminal element because they're exposed to little else.

In this book, Sylvester shows us the value of listening. Through the words and actions of young people he's served and others, he's attempting to show us how we can take the "criminal" out of young people's endeavors. This book shows us how we can help make a Steve Jobs from the "hood." It details how, as we move further and further into the world of technology, entrepreneurship is a real, viable option for kids—especially those who have that communication skill I mentioned, that ability to sell themselves and/or services or products.

What I like about Sylvester's approach is that everything he's writing about is based on the here-and-now. Through food, his students are taught to explore can-do opportunities today, not after college or in adulthood. I predict that "Learning to Listen" will become a valuable addition to anyone's library. For me, it serves as a model for uplifting young people. It's an in-your-face testament to what they deal with while growing up poor. It's a resource chocked full of tried and true examples of people, programs and organizations working to help at-risk youth overcome overwhelming obstacles.

This book can serve as a replicable resource that will hopefully inspire politicians, educators and stakeholders to reevaluate the possibilities and potential of discarded children. I sincerely believe my good friend has managed to create something that can change the negative trajectory of far too many kids while simultaneously addressing social and economic disparities.

Personally, I'd like to see SPP continue to grow and generate applicable ideas on how to revitalize economically-deprived communities all around the country. Most of the proceeds from this book will help fund the Sweet Potato Project. Hopefully, this will serve an extra incentive to buy the book and support a man with a valuable mission in motion.

Sincerely,

Chef Jeff Henderson

INTRODUCTION

Learning to Listen

Photo by Chuck Ramsey

"Mr. Brown, you don't listen."

I must admit, I was a bit taken aback by the letter sent to me by a student I had just fired. She and her younger brother were among the first students to join the Sweet Potato Project (SPP) in 2012. From the beginning, I recognized this young woman's talents. Yeah, she talked too much in class, she was easily distracted and seemed always at-the-ready for verbal combat with seemingly little provocation. But she was an excellent communicator, she shined in front of cameras and she demonstrated strong leadership potential.

"I'm the boss, damnit! You're supposed to do what I say," I thought while reading her letter. How could she say I wasn't listening when I warned both her and her brother about their disruptive behaviors on way too many occasions? I fired her brother because he threatened to body slam me after I chastised him for acting out in class. She was let go after her mother and older sister came to class determined to dress me down. If her mother defended her children's disrespectful behavior, there was very little I could do to help them, I figured.

Still, her letter had an impact. I eventually took the "not listening" part as a message. I called the young lady and we talked. Through our conversation, I learned that her younger brother had become an avid mixed martial arts (MMA) competitor in school. As I listened, I learned the brother was grappling with self-esteem issues and aggression was his way of coping. The young man's girlfriend was pregnant, and he was under a lot of stress. His sister confided that she was on an attention deficit disorder medication. If she ever missed her dosage she was, in her words, "a hot mess."

That simple conversation underscored a few valuable points for me.

1) Many kids, especially at-risk youth, don't always have the necessary skills to articulate what's going on in their worlds.

2) Anybody who's educating, mentoring or dealing with young people must work overtime to understand the background influences affecting their lives.

3) We must develop strategic, effective methods that allow us to see past in-your-face, seemingly confrontational behaviors and tap into the inherent potential of youth.

4) We must develop programs aimed at getting at-risk youth to trust us, open up, share their burdens, hopes and fears and validate their sense of self-worth and identity.

5) We must constantly and continuously work to listen.

This book is dedicated to those highlighted points and more. It is written for anyone involved with shaping the lives of young people, especially low-income or "at-risk" youth. It is for those who develop programs for this fragile demographic. Here, I look at the myriad of challenges confronting young people and offer best case examples and ideas regarding programs and efforts to address their everyday obstacles. I stress the importance of looking, listening and learning what our youth are trying to say through words, behaviors, frustrations and actions.

My subtitle speaks to "recognizing the potential of urban youth." I say this because, in many ways, their lives mirror my upbringing and areas of expertise. However, on a broader scale, America has done itself a disservice by not listening to the cries of all youth who speak out or act out against injustice, inhumanity, gun violence, war, greed, inequality and political malfeasance.

I'm not a psychoanalyst, child psychologist or an educational expert. I am a life-long journalist, an observer, communicator and community activist. I'm a guy with a strong passion for children, especially those who share my hue and my impoverished childhood. Lastly, I'm an old dude determined to "make a difference" before leaving this planet. My biggest contribution to date is SPP, a grassroots program aimed at helping young, urban youth become entrepreneurs in their own neighborhoods.

Still, as fulfilling as this endeavor is, it's extremely challenging. I have always visited young people in schools, churches and even our local juvenile detention center. I have researched and written about the challenges African Americans and young people face for decades. After starting the Sweet Potato Project in 2012, I learned how much I didn't know about marginalized, black youth. Being with them, face-to-face every summer for 10 weeks these past seven years has convinced me that having a good, grassroots entreprenurial program is not enough. Working with young, black kids has exposed me to the hard truths and long-lasting effects of generational poverty, hunger, homelessness, psychic trauma, low sense-of-self, lack of all-encompassing love and more. This was the motivation for writing this book.

I am now in my early sixties. Fundraising has never been one of my strengths. Honestly, I don't know if I'll ever see this program live up to its full potential, which is another reason why I wrote this book. I want to leave something behind that will perhaps inspire the "concerned and connected" to begin or increase programs that address our young people's unique talents, needs and dire circumstances.

It is my humble hope that this book, When We Listen, will motivate us all to try harder to comprehend and address the myriad of issues our kids grapple with daily. I want readers to go beyond the stereotypes and understand the potential of the youth we, as a society, unceremoniously dismiss, deny, lock up and lock out of opportunities.

My wish is that all of us who are determined to intervene in young people's lives consider alternative, unique, effective and grassroots methods to whittle away at the mountainous wedges that mute their chances for success, opportunities, happiness and hope.

Truly listening has reinforced for me the inherent genius, resiliency and creativity of our fragile, marginalized youth. You will read about some who have faced insurmountable, unimaginable odds. Yet, they still manage to do well in school, come up with creative, common sense solutions and still dare to dream.

As I wrote this introduction, protests were again brewing on the streets of St. Louis. As it was in Ferguson in 2014, the judicial outcome of yet another police shooting instigated acts of civil disobedience. It matters not if we agree or disagree with their reasons. What matters is that we listen, which most authoritarian figures fail to do. Oftentimes, adults, myself included, think we know what's best for kids without seeking their input. Media pundits tirelessly work to divert our attention to the sensational: vandalism; angry, seemingly militant black voices; or the way protesters disrupt business or traffic. Most pay no attention to their acts of sheer bravery, their creative tenacity or the fact that they have the audacity to believe they can change a broken system.

Scholarly assessments or studies after high-profile acts of injustice offer valuable input into ways we can offset economic, criminal justice and social inequities. However, what I personally find lacking is a blueprint or an agenda that directly empowers young and low-income people to be the onus of change in the neighborhoods and communities in which they live.

Job training, job fairs, police reform efforts and appeals to major corporations to hire more black youth are indeed necessary. But as statistics bear out, many at-risk, impoverished youth disproportionately drop out of high school. Some have criminal records for minor infractions. Others, especially young women, already have a child or children. These factors may hamper their abilities to ever attend expensive colleges or enter a corporation's door. These issues, however, shouldn't result in permanent poverty, unemployment or early, preventable deaths.

I contend that there is another uncharted area of personal and community empowerment. What if we were to challenge groups like Black Lives Matter to come up with solutions that address the influences that fuel violent interactions with police, like poverty and unemployment? Protesters have painted murals on boarded-up buildings, written brilliant protest songs or poetry, and created t-shirts and other forms of protest art. What if we economically empowered them to start their own businesses and come up with ways to address centuries-old disparities?

At the Sweet Potato Project, we teach kids to grow, market and sell fresh food grown in their neighborhoods. What if some of the 8,000-plus vacant lots in our city were gifted to some of these young people to grow food? What if the thousands upon thousands who want to support young people simply committed to buying their food and food-based products?

My idea is but one idea. As you read further, you will see other bold and creative attempts to salvage and empower young people through innovative approaches.

Dear reader, I have seen the genius of youth far too many of us take for granted. You will read about their challenges, accomplishments and hopes to do better, be better and create opportunities for their parents, peers and neighborhoods. Hopefully, you will agree that they are born survivors with an entrepreneurial edge. They deserve our dead-level best in providing unique and do-able solutions and opportunities for their futures.

If we learn to listen and act on what they're trying to tell us, I have no doubt that the change we all seek will rise like a born-again phoenix with unlimited potential and possibilities.

Sylvester Brown, Jr.

CHAPTER ONE

When They Scream

"You do all this protesting, you do all this marching, and you want to see change. We have yet to see change for the justice system in our country. We're just tired and fed up."

—Clarence from HuffPost "Listen to America" series

Photo Courtesy of the Sweet Potato Project

Our kids are trying to tell us something.

Maybe their pleas are reflected in their actions. It might explain why more than 1 million youth, mostly Black and Latino, drop out of high school every year. There's an obvious gap in our communication with young people when they feel compelled to use guns and kill other young people in schools or on the streets. We must be missing something when the largest percentage of heroin users, according to the Centers for Disease Control (CDC), are kids between the ages of 18 and 25. The fact that 15 percent of the deaths of kids in that age group are drug or alcohol-related is an indicator that we're not communicating properly with our youth.

Perhaps the fact that we're not responding to their needs explains why over 70,000 kids are locked up in juvenile corrections facilities on any given day, according to the Campaign for Youth Justice. Maybe, just maybe, the fact that thousands of young people have taken to the streets to challenge police violence underscores the fact that we adults aren't really tuned into what's really eating them up inside or literally killing them.

Through the Sweet Potato Project, I have listened to the young souls behind biased and sensationalized media headlines. I work with youth from neighborhoods that have been abandoned by middle class families and family-owned businesses and rocked by community disinvestment and illegal drug activity. Most live in a great void created by decades of disregard and disrespect.

Several of my students have lost siblings or loved ones to gun violence. Others are psychologically wounded by how they are perceived, stereotyped and punished. Are we adults cognizant of how these perceptions make them feel about themselves and their neighborhoods? Surrounded by negativity, hopelessness and contradictory messages, many inner-city youth have been robbed of their ability to dream or succeed. In a world where their voices are unheard, it's little wonder why disruptive behavior has become their chosen outlet.

Most kids feel misunderstood by adults. It's natural for older generations to be totally out-of-touch with younger ones. However, the danger, the threat to life is more real to an urban youth who's constantly perceived as criminal, inherently violent or predestined for failure.

Black kids hear the same clichés as white kids. They are told that working hard, persevering, getting a good education and following the rules equates to automatic success. They are told to trust the police and that the criminal justice system is impartial, colorblind and just.

A child development study published in 2017 found that this belief in meritocracy, the notion that individual merit is always rewarded, has an adverse effect on marginalized youth. Erin Godfrey, the study's lead author and an assistant professor of applied psychology at New York University's Steinhardt School explained why the "bootstrap theory" leads to a decline in self-esteem and an increase in risky behaviors for some demographics and not others:

> "If you're in an advantaged position in society, believing the system is fair and that everyone could just get ahead if they just tried hard enough, doesn't create any conflict for you … [you] can feel good about how [you] made it. But for those marginalized by the system—economically, racially, and ethnically—believing the system is fair puts them in conflict with themselves and can have negative consequences."

Godfrey's findings expand on previous studies exploring "system justification," a social psychological theory that explains why humans "tend to defend, bolster, or rationalize the status quo." System justification, Godfrey explained, is a distinct American concept bolstered by age-old myths created to justify inequities. These beliefs can be a liability for disadvantaged adolescents once their identity as a member of a marginalized group begins to gel and they become keenly aware of how institutional discrimination disadvantages them and/or their group.

"'*If the system is fair, why am I seeing that everybody who has brown skin is in this kind of job?*' You're having to think about that," Godfrey explained. He further described how disadvantaged, middle school youth try to rationalize meritocracy. "[It's] like you're not as good, or your social group isn't as good."

I was raised a Jehovah's Witness. My young world was filled with caring, benevolent whites. I visited their homes and hung out with their children. I didn't face racism until my early 20s as an affirmative action hire at a local utility company. Coming face-to-face with oppression based on my skin color rocked my world and sent me spiraling into self-destructive and depraved behavior. Going back to school, falling in love with books and information about my history and starting my own news magazine, Take Five, in 1987 helped get me on a holistic path of knowledge and servitude.

Like it was for me, it's hard for urban youth to articulate the pain and betrayal they feel when myths are contradicted by reality. Most black boys aren't told that police see them as dangerous adults. According to research published by the American Psychological Association, black boys as young as 10 are perceived to be older, seen as guilty for possible crimes more often and face police violence if they are accused of any infraction large or small. One of the authors of the study, University of California professor Phillip Atiba Goff, PhD, expounded on this theory:

"Our research found that black boys can be seen as responsible for their actions at an age when white boys still benefit from the assumption that children are essentially innocent."

In classrooms across the country, black students are far more likely to face harsher discipline than students of other races. A 2012 Department of Education study revealed an uneven system of discipline based on the presumption of a black kid's guilt.

Back in 2013, one of my students, Nadia, then a 19-year-old, fast-talking dreamer anxious to tackle the world told the class about "the jump-out-boys." These are plainclothes St. Louis policemen who specifically patrol "hot spot," violent neighborhoods. Nadia described how these cops constantly harassed her and her friends as they walked the streets or simply hung out in their neighborhoods. Other students chimed in, explaining how these officers jump out of unmarked cars, stop them and purposely try to provoke them with insults and racial expletives while rummaging through their pockets in search of illegal contraband.

It was clear to me that the assumption of guilt, invasion of privacy and intimidating tactics of the "jump-out-boys" damaged Nadia's sense of dignity and fair play. This betrayal of what black kids, since childhood, have been taught about benevolent policemen is something that many can't lucidly express. But the pain percolates in their souls like steaming, stale coffee.

I will never forget the day, also in 2013, when news broke of George Zimmerman's exoneration in the shooting of 17-year-old Trayvon Martin. My students came to class visibly shaken. There was no joking or teasing one another. Their words echoed a deep disappointment of a sad reality. For them, there was no reasonable explanation as to why Zimmerman, a grown, armed neighborhood watchman who was told by police to "stand down," was found innocent after shooting an unarmed teenager.

Like Trayvon, my students wander into unfamiliar neighborhoods.

They, too, eat Skittles or drink Arizona Iced Tea. The "not guilty" verdict was just another systematic assault on their innocence that most had trouble reconciling or adequately verbalizing.

Police brutality is an ongoing discussion in our classes. To address these concerns, we have high-ranking, mostly black officers come to class and talk candidly with our students. They discuss ways to interact with police and resolve seemingly unjust issues. As honest, friendly and engaging as these officers have been, it's still hard for our students to reconcile what they are told with what actually happens to those who look like them.

Many have siblings around the age of 12-year-old Tamir Rice, the Cleveland, Ohio youth shot by police on November 22, 2014 while holding a toy gun. It doesn't matter where we adults stand on Tamir's perceived guilt or innocence. Rationalizing or talking about police bias or their inability to gauge the age of black kids doesn't douse the internal fire of a kid who knows Tamir was shot dead in less than 2 seconds after police arrived on the scene.

Protesting police violence is just one way and one issue that makes our kids metaphorically and literally scream. Far too many tune out in classrooms where teachers who don't share their pigmentation devalue their culture or underestimate their potential. Our youth must bear the burden of their lives screened through muddied, stereotypical lenses. They are aware of how "outsiders" view them and the neighborhoods of their origin. Well-meaning teachers who tell them they must get a "good education to escape the ghetto," have no idea that they're dissing young people's parents, friends and the places many revere as home.

***

In his March 2015 TEDTALK, Rev. Jeffrey Brown, one of the architects of the "Boston miracle" where the city cut youth violence by more 65 percent, described the first step to recovery. "Listen to those kids, don't just preach to them, and help them reduce violence in their own neighborhoods," Brown advised.

The reverend's words reinforce my belief that we can instigate positive change by listening to young people, no matter how uncomfortable their words or actions make us feel.

The first couple of weeks of our summer program is dedicated to creating a comfort zone where kids can share the frustrations of their worlds. I've found this to be a difficult task. Black kids today seem to have adopted the mantra of our ancestors. They think they have to be tough and hard and they diligently try to keep painful feelings bottled up.

> *"Listen to those kids, don't just preach to them, and help them reduce violence in their own neighborhoods."*—Rev. Jeffrey Brown

One effective tool we utilize is our news round-up session where every morning students are mandated to share a recent news story. Ironically, most recite ghastly accounts of crime and violence locally or nationally. Stories of murder, robberies, rape or gang violence instigate "me too" moments where students get personal about incidents they've experienced or that have taken the lives of relatives or friends. Without putting them on the spot, the news-sharing exercise allows them to voice their feelings in a safe, nonjudgmental, open environment.

During the first couple weeks of our program we look for ways to get our students to open up, talk publicly and express their feelings.

We also do this through skits, poetry, art and exercises that allow them to verbalize or act out their feelings. Through these drills, students develop a comfortable kinship with their peers and they're reminded that they're not alone.

Elesha, a 2012 SPP student, perfectly summed up our engagement practices: "Speaking and performing in front of our peers was important because Mr. Brown wanted to first see our individual talents and, second, he wanted us to be comfortable around our peers and to just loosen up and be ourselves."

In 2014, I interviewed some of our students between the ages of 16 and 19 at that time. My goal was to hear their challenges in their own words. Myke, one of our first-year students, helped me understand why black youth experience difficulty articulating their feelings: "A lot of young African Americans are really shallow. They don't like to share feelings or emotions. They'll talk about the new Jordans coming out, or the new video games, stuff like that. But they don't want to get really deep into how they feel."

We've found that some of our students harbor deep disappointment or resentment toward their own neighborhoods or adults in general. Myke also spoke to this self-loathing tendency: "I've noticed over the years that African Americans degrade themselves more and more as time goes on. You'll notice that at parties or gatherings. As a people, we've degraded ourselves to a point where we don't even want to hear 'you can do it.' We don't want to believe that."

I asked the students to describe their environments. Another student, Darryeon, was struck by the types of businesses he sees in in low-income neighborhoods like his: "There are so many check-cashing places because people think it's the quickest place to cash their checks instead of using banks. They buy lottery tickets and liquor because they probably think those are important things. The store-owners think about what people want instead of focusing on the kids or making our communities better."

Barry, expanded on Darryeon's observations: "So, if you're poor and think you have no options, a sign promoting the lottery means 'hope.' It's a way to get immediate gratification. Also, like tobacco and stuff, people are always looking for ways to love themselves up, sort of speak."

Marquitta addressed the subliminal impact of advertising in poor neighborhoods: "All we really see are signs and stuff about liquor and tobacco products. That's not doing anything but influencing and encouraging people to keep buying those things. It feeds the mindset that it's a dream you can have."

One of our younger students at the time, Keon, Marquitta's cousin, flipped the script and spoke to the kinds of businesses he'd like to see in black neighborhoods: "We need more family-owned stores, places where you can bring your kids. If you're from out-of-town and visiting your family, you have to stay in a hotel downtown because of how bad North St. Louis is. We need better businesses, not the kind where the liquor store's signs are brighter than a cross on a church."

> "We need better businesses, not the kind
> where the liquor stores signs are brighter than
> a cross on a church."

When the discussion turned to minority student's disproportionate high school dropout rates, the students shared even more valuable insights. Darria (not her real name), a student we recruited from the juvenile detention center in 2012, was candid about her experiences at school. She was diagnosed as bipolar at an early age and told me about her struggles with low self-esteem: "It made me feel like I can't do nuthin, that I'm slow, I'm dumb and stuff like that. But I know I'm not. When teachers talk down to me, I feel like I have to prove myself, show them that I'm smart and intelligent. I don't know why but I just do."

Darria used her experiences to tell me why other kids might fall through the cracks: "They probably drop out because they're having problems at home or having problems learning at school. They probably have challenges like me. I have trouble reading and I'm afraid to read in front of people. Adults don't know how to talk to you and some kids don't know either. So, it might make you angry or set you off."

Barry elaborated: "You have to look at the situation at home. Some African Americans don't even have a home. All that stuff counts and has a major impact on us. If you hear all this yapping and what-not about getting an education, then you go to school...even if you're trying to do good, it's going to make you not want to go."

Charles, another first-year SPP student, was pessimistically honest about pursuing higher education: "School is not for me. I can do it, but I don't see myself graduating from high school then jumping right into college. I really don't feel school. It educated me and got me ready for the real world, I guess. But I've been branded. Even though I'm doing good, I get branded as a trouble-maker. When something goes wrong, they automatically blame me...I don't like that."

> *"I get branded as a trouble-maker. When something goes wrong, they automatically blame me...I don't like that."*

Marquitta spoke to the frustrations students like Charles or Darria may have with school. "To be honest, I think most African American kids drop out because they feel like school is overwhelming or they just can't do it," she said, adding "It's probably because they don't put their minds to it as much as they should. Most black kids have been around violence all their life so that creates problems for them, too."

I was curious about the attraction to illegal drug sales. Charles helped me better understand how such a dangerous entity is still alluring to many young people. "I don't know about other people, but money is a big deal to me," he explained. "Some kids just need money or they're tired of depending on their parents. They just want to be out there making money. It's a faster way. Some were probably brought up around drugs, so if they can see a way to make their own money, that's what they're going to do. They see other people get the money, the cars and everything, so they want it, too."

***

"What do you want from us?"

During a 2011 town hall meeting on youth violence called "Pass the Mic," moderator Rev. Vickie Caldwell asked audience members under 25, "What do you want from us?"

The meeting was convened five days after two teenagers were killed outside a local nightclub on Christmas night. The gathering at St. John's United Church of Christ in North St. Louis was orchestrated to help young people openly discuss the region's alarmingly high murder rate.

It's clear adults have "failed somewhere," Rev. Caldwell said before encouraging the crowd of 200 or so to fill in the gaps for adults.

Apparently, the young folk had lots to say. For almost four hours, they asked adults to come out of their comfort zones, volunteer or become mentors and role models and more. As the meeting drew to its conclusion, dozens of young people were still lined up to offer more recommendations.

Malik Ahmed, founder and CEO of Better Family Life, Inc., encouraged the audience to be honest, look within and seek common goals that benefit the community. "We have to be honest with ourselves," Ahmed said. "We lack a collective purpose and harmony among each other. We have got to have a deeper purpose."

A major part of the recovery and redress process, Rev. Brown stressed, is "listening." If we are to truly help students (black, white or "other") be the best they can possibly be and become change-agents who will revitalize long-ignored communities, we must truly hear their concerns, frustrations, desires and hopes. We must understand that our modern educational approaches need to incorporate young people's current conditions, their hopes and fears and the overwhelming impact of being viewed as dangerous, expendable and less-than.

After listening, however, we must act. Caring and concerned adults must step back and analyze how our schools, our police and our society contributes to feelings of low self-worth and low self-esteem. Understanding how poor, black kids are labeled at early ages may help us create neighborhood, church or community alternative programs specifically designed to help them see themselves as the vessels of potential that they are truly meant to be.

REFLECTION

Celebrity Chef Fires up
Youth in Juvenile Detention Center

by Sylvester Brown, Jr.

Originally published May 7, 2012 — http://sylvesterbrownjr.blogspot.com/

Photo Courtesy of the Sweet Potato Project

"Why you muggin' me?"

"I ain't mugging you, man," the sullen youth dressed in a red sweat suit responded.

For a moment it seemed as if Chef Jeff Henderson was about to deliver a bit of tough love on the insolent teen as we gathered inside the St. Louis Juvenile Detention Center.

"I don't have to be here," Henderson shouted, stepping closer to the boy, "I'm here on my own dime and all I'm asking is 30 minutes to talk to you."

While visiting St. Louis for a speaking engagement, Henderson, author of the New York Times best-selling memoir, *Cooked:*

From the Streets to the Stove, from Cocaine to Foie Gras (William Morrow) conducted a 4-hour cooking presentation with some of the youth at the center. Chef Jeff, a former drug dealer who spent 10 years in jail for his crimes, makes a priority to visit juvenile detention centers to uplift and inspire youth with his turn-around story.

The encounter with the seemingly angry boy occurred about two hours after Henderson's cooking session. Earlier that day, six young people—five boys and one girl—were chosen to help prepare the evening meal for the other young detainees and staff. The menu for that evening consisted of Henderson's famous fried chicken, mashed potatoes and corn on the cob. The small group dressed in color-specific sweat suits (red for boys ages 16-17, green for boys ages 12-15 and yellow for girls) were asked to circle the celebrity chef.

"OK, who's the boss?" Henderson asked before starting.

Although a couple of hands inched up, it became clear as the day progressed that Darria (not her real name), a girl with a no-nonsense frown and attitude to match, was the alpha dog of the group. Henderson seemed to pick up on this early and focused extra attention on the girl, putting her in charge of the kitchen crew.

"You let them know what you need," he said, placing his hand on the Darria's shoulder. "You guys are a team, you need to communicate."

The exercise was a mini demonstration of the mantra Henderson shares with Fortune 500 companies, financial and learning institutions, culinary and technical schools, state and federal corrections and social service agencies around the country. The chef believes that everyone, including people from troubled backgrounds, have the potential to be productive and successful. The skills that allowed him to run a million-dollar, illegal empire in the 1980s, he says, are the same skills that helped him succeed in the culinary and corporate worlds. The key, Henderson preaches, is "changing the product."

Within a half hour, the kids were humming along like a seasoned kitchen crew—cutting, boiling and mashing potatoes, shucking corn and dropping floured drum sticks into bubbling hot grease. The chef wasn't hesitant to correct the youth as they performed their tasks. "Stand up straight. Quit talking. You can't slouch and run your mouths on a real job. Remember, smile. No one wants a frowning worker," Henderson said while also adding heavy doses of compliments. "That'll work. Thank you. Good job crew," he repeated often.

"Who wants to be the taster?" The chef asked after the first batch of hot chicken came out of the fryer.

The kids shouted, "me, me, me!"

Henderson again placed his hand on Darria's shoulder. "My assistant manager here, she'll be the taster."

For the first time that day, I noticed the girl's brilliant, white-toothed smile.

Pugh Jaunell, the young, muscled counselor who oversees the boys, noticed something different about the kids. He hadn't had to check any on their behavior that day, "which is unusual," he told me.

"They're actually paying attention, which is again, unusual," Jaunell added.

Nikeisha Fortenbery, assistant program coordinator, was equally impressed with the performance of Henderson's six helpers. She commented on the smiles most of the kids displayed as they hustled around the kitchen.

"This was great for them," Fortenbery told me. "They're smiling because, today, they can see themselves differently. They were allowed to actually use their talents and create something they can share with their friends."

Two hours later, the food was ready and placed on large, metal, gray trays. The six kids lined up behind the chow line served the food. The other detainees, also dressed in red and green (Darria was the only girl that day), filed in. Each of the boys entered with their hands behind their backs as if handcuffed. Apparently, they'd been told to walk this way in groups.

The young detainees who were summoned to the chow line table-by-table, along with the staff, consumed the food with great gusto. Henderson stood before the entire group after dinner. He called the six young workers to the front of the room and demanded that the well-fed group thank the food-preparers for their hard work. The young workers smiled sheepishly among the modest applause.

"I'm so proud of my babies," Ms. Gerry, the center's cook, said. "They're really enjoying this. They're getting the attention they need. This will be a lasting experience for them."

After the acknowledgements, Henderson began to address the group. Earlier, he had noticed a skinny, 10-year-old boy among the detainees. He had the child sit close to him as he shared his story of crime, redemption and unprecedented success with the group. Some of the other hardened boys didn't seem particularly impressed with Henderson's story. This was the point where the chef confronted the boy he accused of "mugging" him.

Instead of berating the teen further, Henderson asked Nathan Graves, the detention center's program coordinator, to play the DVD he'd brought along. It opened with Oprah Winfrey praising Chef Jeff for overcoming obstacles and turning his life around. Images on the

DVD showed Henderson as a drug dealer, a convict, and later as a chef working at some the finest restaurants in the country, including the Marriot, Ritz Carlton, Hotel Bel-Air, L'Ermitage, Caesar's Palace and the Bellagio Hotel where he became the first African-American executive chef at the prestigious establishment.

Somehow the video made Henderson's story more real for the youth. They seemed to pay rapt attention to every word. After the DVD ended, the chef segued into raw and real dialogue about prison as the destination for people who make poor choices. He urged the kids to examine their weaknesses and mistakes, build on their unique gifts and abandon "homies" or activities that may cause them to wind up in this or other criminal justice facilities.

"A smart man listens to wise advice. An ignorant fool doesn't," Henderson lectured.

One could only marvel at the transformation of the six kitchen helpers and most of the boys in just under four hours.

"These kids are looking for discipline and an adult who'll be straight with them," Henderson told me earlier. "They're just like you and me, they have big dreams and ambitions. They want opportunities but, sadly, they come from neighborhoods were dreams are dashed and opportunities are few."

As the presentation ended and the boys were leaving the dining hall, Henderson pulled the smart-alecky teen aside for personal consult. Attitude gone, the boy asked the chef how he could contact him. Henderson gave him his card and promised he'd visit the juvenile center again.

It was obvious that a light bulb of possibilities had clicked on in the minds of the youthful attendees. Unfortunately, Chef Jeff can't stay with kids he motivates around the country. More than likely, that bulb will be quickly dimmed by the overwhelming negative influences in their lives, neighborhoods and environments. I couldn't help but wonder: what would happen if, as Ms. Gerry mentioned, the youth constantly received the attention they need?

One of the counselors brought Darria to me after the presentation. Henderson had told a few staff members that I planned to start a summer program for at-risk youth in North St. Louis.

"This young lady has so much potential," the counselor told me.

Darria jotted down her mother's name and phone number on my yellow note pad. The young lady, whom I first considered hard, exhibited a shy smile and a plea for opportunity.

"Call me. I really need to do something, please."

CHAPTER TWO
When They Are Labeled

"Look in the dictionary and the synonyms of the word 'black.' It's always something degrading and low and sinister. Look at the word 'white,' it's always something pure, high and clean. Well, I want to get the language right tonight. I want to get the language so right that everybody here will cry out; Yes, I'm black and I'm proud of it, yes I'm black and beautiful!"

—Dr. Martin Luther King, Jr.

Photo by Benjamin Gandhi-Shepard

Students Charles and Darria's comments in the previous chapter about being branded as "trouble-makers," or made to feel dumb shouldn't be taken lightly. According to several studies, black students— especially black, male students—are disproportionately labeled and punished far more often than white students who commit the same infractions.

According to a 2015 study by the Civil Rights Project at UCLA, my state, Missouri, has the widest suspension gap between black and white students in the nation. Its state-funded preschools expel children at twice the national rate. Black kindergartners who bite, preschoolers with toileting issues, "aggressive" second-graders and children who start fights or are caught with illegal drugs or weapons are all punished and suspended from public schools at disproportionately higher rates than white kids who commit the same transgressions.

The *St. Louis Post-Dispatch* noted the punishment disparities in Missouri schools. In affluent Kirkwood, where black students made up about 14 percent of the district's enrollment in 2014, those students constituted 71 percent of all suspensions. Black children in the Ferguson-Florissant district made up 80 percent of enrollment but accounted for 92 percent of suspensions. In the majority white Lindbergh School District, black students only represented 4 percent of the student body but garnered16 percent of suspensions.

Most of the elementary suspensions in Missouri happen in cash-strapped school districts with high concentrations of children struggling academically, socially and economically, according to the *Post-Dispatch*. Most over-worked and under-paid teachers in these districts haven't received the proper training to help them identify or effectively cope with what they perceive as "problematic behaviors."

"They're the children being overly suspended and kept out," Amanda Schneider, an attorney with Legal Services of Eastern Missouri, told *Post-Dispatch* educational reporter Elisa Crouch. Schneider's clients include parents of suspended children. "They're low-income clients. They're in poverty. They have children who need intensive services and support," she explained.

Another 2015 study by researchers at Stanford University found that teachers may not only judge the behavior of black students more harshly than white pupils, but they were also more likely to view them as "troublemakers." "The fact that black children are disproportionately disciplined in school is beyond dispute," said psychologist and Stanford University Professor Jennifer Eberhardt.

The issue is further complicated by a society that's willing to spend more money on incarcerating minority youth than educating them. In 2016, the Department of Education released a startling report of our country's spending on prisons versus public schools. The report showed that every state spends less on pre-k–12th grade education than they do on correction facilities. It further noted that state and local spending on public colleges and universities over the past 20 years remained stagnant while spending on prison systems, including private prisons, rose by 90 percent.

Additionally, according to the DoED report, public and charter schools that have predominantly Black or Hispanic student populations tend to have higher rates of discipline against students of color.

These reports indicate that stereotyping motivates many teachers to interpret and punish students specifically based on their skin color. Many experts say that this troublesome mindset sets black children on a course that fuels the "pre-school-to-prison-pipeline." As children move up in grades, so do their records of punishment and suspensions. Teachers who can't deal with problem behaviors punish based on their perceptions and biases. Oftentimes, they are not trained to identify environmental triggers that hamper a child's ability to learn or behave in school. Students from some of the most violent neighborhoods are expected to behave like students who hail from safer, upper or middle-class environments.

What's not acknowledged nearly enough is the long-lasting psychological impact labeling has on young people of color. Patrick Sharkey, Ph.D., a sociologist from New York University, found that children's scores on vocabulary and reading tests fall days after a homicide happens in their neighborhoods. Many public schools are not equipped to address emotions related to death, fear or anxiety, Sharkey noted. Yet violence has a long-term effect on school performance.

Lisa Delpit, MacArthur Foundation award-winner and author of *Other People's Children*, claims that low educational performance of black students can also be directly attributed to a "deeply ingrained bias of equating blackness with inferiority."

At tender ages, Delpit said, "black students undergo a series of microaggressions...small psychic insults that debilitate them." Young black males perform poorly, she added, because they have internalized negative stereotypes. Sometimes, Delpit continued, "black students are invisible, unnoticed and disrespected, and sometimes they are hyper-visible, [having] their normal youth behaviors magnified into pathologies. They end up estranged from school culture, mistrusting their own capacities and fulfilling belittling expectations."

Black students are invisible, unnoticed and disrespected, and sometimes they are hyper-visible, [having] their normal youth behaviors magnified into pathologies. They end up estranged from school culture, mistrusting their own capacities and fulfilling belittling expectations."

Because the behavior of black students has been undiagnosed and untreated, many grow up to have negative encounters with employers and fellow employees, police officers, and once they're in "the system," prison guards and prisoners. In many cases, this vicious cycle starts when a child is suspended from school in early grades.

***

Too Important to Fail

I started the Sweet Potato Project after working with SmileyBooks, a book company founded by former PBS commentator, Tavis Smiley. I was blessed to serve as a consultant, researcher and contributor on several books and projects under his label. One book, *Too Important to Fail,* and one PBS special, "Education Under Arrest," both written or hosted by Tavis Smiley, opened my eyes to the challenges young people face in America's public-school systems.

While working on *Too Important to Fail,* for example, I learned that a disproportionate number of ineffective and unqualified teachers are assigned to low-income schools. A 2010 Education Trust report titled "Not Prepared for Class: High-Poverty Schools Continue to Have Fewer In-Field Teachers," found that students in low-income communities are routinely taught by unqualified teachers.

Through my work on Tavis' PBS special, "Education Under Arrest," I also learned that America's schools serve as key entry points to the juvenile justice system. One in three of every teen arrested are arrested in school. Because of draconian "Zero Tolerance" polices initiated after the horrifying 1999 Columbine shooting, kids are arrested, kicked out or drop out of schools the first time they transgress. "Education Under

Arrest" presented these startling statistical facts:

68% of all urban high schools now have police patrolling their corridors.

Most in the juvenile justice system are there for non-violent crimes.

Two-thirds to three-fourths of teens who have been incarcerated drop out of high school.

This means that even minor offenses, such as disruptive behavior, foul language or truancy result in suspensions, expulsions or arrests. In other words, offenses that were once handled in schools with parents are now automatic criminal offenses. This, experts say, shoves mostly black kids into the insidious juvenile justice system where punishment takes precedent over rehabilitation or re-integration into schools.

"Education Under Arrest" also looked at what's working to counter the devastatingly high number of kids arrested at schools for infractions that, years ago, would have resulted in a visit to the principal's office or a call to parents. Officials dedicated to keeping kids in school and reforming the educational and criminal justice systems boldly spoke out in the book. One example was Jimmie Edwards, a St. Louis Juvenile Court Judge, founder of Innovative Concept Academy and a strong advocate for alternative education.

The "Safe Schools Act" is Missouri's equivalent of the national zero-tolerance initiative. Since its passage in 1999, Edwards said, the law has not only had a devastating impact on children—particularly poor and minority youth—but it renders educators useless. "It has taken away the opportunity of school administrators and various superintendents to address discipline within the state's school districts. It has allowed the system to pass the buck onto the courts and, unfortunately, when children are put in court systems they are treated like criminals."

As an appointed juvenile justice judge, Edwards said he can scrutinize and offer options to the country's "lock 'em up and throw away the key mentality." Mass incarceration of children, he explained, only feeds the insatiable criminal justice system. He explains, "you take an 11 or 12-year-old and lock them up for an hour, a day or two days because they possessed marijuana and that child will know more about criminality when he gets out than he would have ever known in a lifetime. He now knows more about marijuana, how to cook crack cocaine, how to make methamphetamine and how to load an assault weapon. These are things he learned *inside* the system."

According a 2011 Children's Defense Fund study, "Portrait of Inequality," the pre-school to prison pipeline represents a national crisis for black youth. Here are more grim statistics:

- Nationally, Black youth are more than four times as likely as white youth to be detained in a juvenile correctional facility. About two-thirds are detained for nonviolent offenses.

- In 2008, Blacks constituted 17 percent of the youth population (age 10 to 17), yet they constituted 31 percent of all juvenile arrests.

- Between the ages of 10 and 17, Black youth are five times as likely as white youth to be arrested for a violent crime.

- Black males born in 2001 are more than five times as likely as white males to be incarcerated at some time in their lifetime.

- Black males age 18 and over in 2008 represented only five percent of the total college student population, but 36 percent of the total prison population.

Michelle Alexander, author of the highly acclaimed book *The New Jim Crow: Mass Incarceration in the Age of Colorblindness*, wrote that "there are more African Americans under correctional control, whether in prison or in jail, on probation or on parole, than there were enslaved in the year 1850." During a March 2010 interview with *Democracy Now,* Alexander said "The rules and laws that govern ghetto communities today and the war that is being waged there ensures that a large majority of black and brown boys will be branded as felons, labeled as criminals, at very young ages, often before they even reach voting age, before they turn eighteen."

The sad truth is, America is stubbornly insistent on locking up its future. The building of new prisons is based on the birthrate of Black and Latino boys. How many statistics can we reduce by creating young, urban entrepreneurs? How many jobs and businesses can we build with youth activated with an entrepreneur's mindset?

If we choose to look beyond acts of perceived insolence or disruptive behavior instead of automatically punishing kids, we may arrive at better programs and policies that will help kids who presumably "act out." Maybe their behavior is another indication that we're not listening or responding to their environmental deficits.

Later, in Chapter Five, "When They Are Traumatized," I speak of the horrific experiences some of my students have endured. Honestly, when I learn of their trials and tribulations, my respect for them increases. Their resiliency, despite tremendous odds, fuels my belief that—with empathy, love, guidance and cultural reinforcement—they can be empowered to overcome the obstacles that place far too many of them on the pathway to prison.

THE CULTURAL DEFICIT: AN INCONVENIENT TRUTH

Nicole Adewala of Abna Construction

I absolutely love it when Nicole Adewale visits our classroom or lets my students come to her business, Abna Engineering. Nicole and her husband, Abe Adewale, co-founded the company in 1994. With more than 70 employees, Abna offers engineering services for civil, structural, geotechnical and transportation projects as well as land surveying, construction management, testing and inspection services. The Adewale's operate in several states including Missouri, Illinois, Arkansas, Louisiana, Oklahoma, Indiana, Michigan, Kansas and Kentucky.

Nicole has the unique ability of breaking down her complex operations into understandable chunks for our students. When we visit her business, students can look at and touch dirt and rock samples and see the process Abna uses to test materials to gauge their suitability for construction projects. Nicole not only serves as a model of a black woman excelling in an intricate field, she's a down-to-earth matriarch who takes the time to explore the lives of our students. No matter what challenges they face, students leave Adewale with a sense of pride, hope and inspiration.

Black professionals, educators and mentors are valuable assets in educating children of color. Black youth need adults in their lives who have lived or are empathetic to their environments. Unfortunately, America's public-school system is woefully lacking in providing teachers of color in its classrooms, especially black male teachers. It is a problem recognized by the National Education Association (NEA). Under the heading "Blacks: Education Issues" on its website, the NEA states: "Recruiting and retaining teachers of color is important, as some children of color will go through their entire educational career without having a teacher who looks like them or who can identify with the uniqueness of their cultural heritage."

"Some children of color will go through their entire educational career without having a teacher who looks like them or who can identify with the uniqueness of their cultural heritage."—National Education Association

Famed educator Dr. Jawanza Kunjufu noted in *Too Important to Fail* that 83 percent of America's teachers are white and female. Since the *Brown vs. Topeka Board of Education* case in 1954, Kunjufu explained that there has been a 66 percent decline in African American teachers, with only one percent of African American males in America's teaching force.

THE SWEET POTATO PROJECT APPROACH:

"Still I'll never know...Why a child is blamed...Ridiculed and shamed...We're all the same..."

— "Ghetto Child" by the Spinners

Alex D. Fennoy VP of
Midwest BankCentre

Fr. Steve Giljum with
St. Catholic Academy

Class presentation with author, artist and
fashion designer, Reginald Forman

Entrepreneur, Chris Bolten

At SPP, we try to introduce our students to as many professional African-Americans as possible. We want them to make personal connections with success. Judging by their written responses, we seem to be on the right track. In their essays, students like Marquitta Williams, who has been with SPP since its inception, found the visits from black professionals motivational. "From each person we met, we got a different character and insights into what it was like when they were younger and how their lives could have been when they were heading down the wrong road," she wrote in 2014. "For me, it was like, 'look what they turned out to be!' Because they put their minds to it, they made something of themselves. Each of them built us up and provided a different look at what's out there and what's possible."

Muhammad Raqib, lead motivator and mentor of "Real Men Talk," a motivational/empowerment organization in the St. Louis region, visited our students in the summer of 2013. He brought slides from his brief stay in Belize in Central America. Raqib wanted to show what extreme poverty looks like in hopes that my students would take advantage of programs like ours. One student, Charles seemed to have gotten the message: "Mr. Raqib brought back pictures where people lived in total garbage. He showed us that there are people much worse off than us and we need to take advantage of stuff in America," Charles said, adding: "He also told us how he used to be a drug dealer and how he came back from that life. He showed us that just as fast as you get into the game you can get out."

It's encouraging that current research is helping educators and institutions take constructive steps to hire more black and male teachers, come up with effective methods to address a student's behavior other than locking them up or locking them out of school through suspensions. But, as Smiley wrote in *Too Important to Fail,* approximately 1.3 million students drop out of high school every year. With an estimated 7,000 students, mostly black and poor, dropping out of classrooms every day, we can ill afford to wait for the educational system to correct itself.

It's beyond question that youth are labeled, misunderstood and punished simply because they are black or brown. There are effective ways to offset the ramifications of this mindset and everyone can play a role. But it's crucial that the black community step up, lead and create alternative programs designed to give their kids extra love, extra validation, more cultural reinforcement and bring professionals into their lives that look like them, know them and can inspire them to proudly compete and beat overwhelming odds.

REFLECTION

Interview with an Educator

by Sylvester Brown, Jr.

January 2018

Tiffany Shawn / Courtesy of Tiffany Shawn

"There will come a time when the national media and celebrities shedding light on the issues go home. Life will go on as usual for some. HOWEVER...The family will still grieve. People will still need jobs. Children will still need ways to remain active. Political decisions will still require your discernment. What will you do then?"—Tiffany Shawn, August 19, 2014

Life literally changed for educator/writer Tiffany Shawn after the police shooting of 18-year-old Michael Brown. Before the shooting, she wrote for her blog, *MyNaturalReality.com* and DELUX Magazine, a small, local publication. Her major areas of focus were travel, hair, fashion and entertainment.

That all changed after August 9, 2014. Shawn heard about the shooting while hanging out with her family. The impact wasn't immediate. In fact, in the wake of such high-profile vigilante or police killings in cases such as Trayvon Martin, 17 (2012), Cary Ball, 25 (April 2013) and Eric Garner, 43 (July 2014), she was initially nonplussed by the news of Mike Brown's death.

"I was with family," Shawn recalls. "When I first heard about it, it was like 'oh, man, police did it again' but it didn't really hit me until three or four days later." What did catch her attention was the location of the shooting. "This murder occurred in part of a district where I graduated high school, five miles away from what was called "ground zero." In addition to that, I grew up, for the most part, in and around the Normandy area, three miles away from where Mike Brown was shot."

Her penchant for journalism and the idea that people were gathering in an area of her youth prompted Shawn to visit "ground zero." She wound up chronicling what would become history-in-the-making for St. Louis' largest black newspaper, The St. Louis American. What struck her most was the blatant brutality of militarized policemen determined to quell the growing protests. "For me," she said, "it was the way they treated people in the streets, especially the tear-gassing. It was like 'this shouldn't be happening. They need more bodies out here.'"

Shawn became an engaged activist and reporter. Two things

became quickly apparent, she told me. First, was the "true sense of community," where she met a diverse group of people with shared interests determined to change something. "Many of my family members were scared for me when I was out there protesting. I didn't have fear necessarily, probably because of those I was with. We had each other's back, everyone was sticking together, watching out for one another."

The second factor tapped into her passions as an educator. Although people of all ages were involved, she was struck by the number of young people targeted, harassed, stereotyped and how the media distorted their images, messages, anger and frustrations. "The disrespect accorded to people of color is just outrageous to me. How can you call someone a 'terrorist' who is not armed, not trying to harm anybody but speaking out against what's harming them?" Shawn recalled. "There's a good portion, but not all, of law enforcement, politicians and people who don't see people of color as people yet. They've yet to step out of slavery, out of the Jim Crow era…they're still stuck in a time way, way back and haven't brought their minds to the fact that, first and foremost, we're all just people."

In her early 30s at the time, Shawn gravitated toward a group of her peers who became mentors and counselors for some of the other young protestors. "We got to know some of the younger guys who were trying to protect their own neighborhoods. They weren't necessarily trying to become activists but, over time, they did. They were able to loudly spread the word of what they wanted people to hear. There were times when me or my friends would pull them aside and say things like, 'I know your message is this, but maybe say it in another way…' we were almost guiding them in a sense."

"Almost" was the operative word. Shawn cautions against acting as "saviors" for young people who are, most times, much more aware of their own circumstances. "If you're trying to help marginalized people, you can't go in like you know more than they do. That's their neighborhood, their streets. You have to come from a place in your heart where you're just trying to assist them in the way that *they* need you. It may not be in the way you expect," Shawn explained. "Through listening, through conversations, through knowing what you're getting into, you'll know how they need your help. We must show them that we're there to help. And, in that sense, we're helping ourselves, too."

Unlike the media's sensationalized reporting of vandalism or looting during the protests, Shawn noted a strong sense of self-discipline, resiliency and creativity among the young protestors. The different strategies employed, the art and cultural expressions that arose from Mike Brown's death were all activities that inspired her.

"Was I impressed? Absolutely!" Shawn said. "These were young people who hadn't done anything like this before. Friends I made like Brittany [Ferrell] and Alexus [Templeton] weren't people who had been planning this their whole lives. They just stepped up in a major way."

Perhaps it was her educator side speaking, but Shawn said helping young people tap into their creativity is a positive way to assist them in expressing their angst and frustrations. "It's a matter of showing them ways to have their voices heard, especially if they're not the ones who'll be out in the open, protesting. We need to show them there are other ways to get it out. You can write poetry, do art and music and still have your message understood."

Shawn said she's lucky to work in a school district that encourages its teachers to write curriculum that's aimed at social awareness. For Shawn, the freedom to wade into complicated racial or social arenas gives her a chance to engage and inspire young minds.

"I'm always going to teach the truth. If we come across something remotely inaccurate, we're going to unpack it and talk about why it's either true, not true, what's the facts or why it happened in the first place," Shawn said, adding that she works hard not to influence or hamper but stimulate critical thought. "I'm very careful not to just give them my viewpoints. I want them to create their own, but I also want them to have the facts and the truth of any situation."

Since the protests of 2014 and 2017, Shawn has given birth to two children, ages two and three months. With her children in mind, the educator/activist/writer takes the long-range view of protesting and changing how black people are treated in this country. "I don't think it will change in my lifetime, but I have to look at history, I have to see that there's been change over time. My grandparents are almost in their 90s and I think about the changes they've seen. I know that what we're doing and the people around me are doing is going to have an impact someday and in some way." If not, Shawn noted, there are two young people for sure who'll know the power of collective responsibility and personal advocacy: "I'm leaving something behind for my children even if it's just the fact that they know their mom didn't sit back and just let things happen."

CHAPTER THREE

When They Belong

"You are the young, urban pioneers who will help revitalize our neighborhoods and create jobs and opportunities for your siblings and peers."

Photo Courtesy of the Sweet Potato Project

This is the message we share with the Sweet Potato Project students every year.

One of the ways we teach awareness and community ownership is through our "Neighborhood Walks." We want students to understand the economic and social dynamics that impact their lives and surrounding neighborhoods. We visit areas in St. Louis that are economically mixed, majority white, majority black or racially diverse.

With notebooks and pens in hand, students visit these different parts of the city. I ask that they look, observe and jot down the types of businesses, advertisements, signs in shop windows and the varying conditions of the neighborhoods we visit. Their reflections are oftentimes disheartening for me. Our students are very candid and critical about the conditions they see in low-income, black neighborhoods.

Consider these essay comments:

On the north side I saw a lot of trash in the street and on the sidewalks. The broken and badly damaged sidewalks make it difficult for elderly and disabled people. Fast food restaurants surrounded the north side area as well as abandoned houses and buildings.-Tytianna

The neighborhoods had liquor stores or churches on almost every corner. I saw a lot of stores and inside almost all was a sign that read 'We accept EBT.' This is where stereotypes come in. I ask myself 'is this what makes a 'hood' a 'hood?-Renesha

I barely saw black-owned businesses. Stores like pay-day loans, auto shops, Chinese Food places and beauty supply stores surround the area. When looking at houses, there was visible damage from weather and the bricks were old and faded. The only visible flowers were weeds growing through cracked sidewalks and the gravel on parking lots.-Keyundra

The people on Grand (southside) were of different races and cultures, all living in the community as one. On Natural Bridge (northside) I saw one race of people, black people, separated from good communities and chances to succeed.— Arthur

***

Their comments underscore the difficulty of our mission. How do we get black kids to take ownership of or work to revitalize poor neighborhoods if they view them negatively? How do you foster a generation of urban entrepreneurs if they look at themselves or their neighborhoods with revulsion or skepticism?

The people on Grand (southside) were of different races and cultures, all living in the community as one. On Natural Bridge (northside) I saw one race of people, black people, separated from good communities and chances to succeed. —SPP student, Arthur

For me, it's a matter of digging deeper. The students spoke glowingly of majority-white neighborhoods or business districts we visited. They love the fact that there's a hotel and concert hall in University City. They marvel at the number of eclectic shops and dining establishments with outdoor seating in the tony Central West End area. They praise the sense of community and safety on the Grand business strip. It was the little things: a sign welcoming all immigrants as patrons, a water park with concrete benches stashed between a pizza joint and a used book store, the light-changing buttons that electronically inform pedestrians when to cross the street.

In contrast, they found their own neighborhoods sorely lacking and deplorable.

Their reactions differed, however, when I asked the kids to describe where they felt most comfortable. The group told me about the visit to the Central West End with its high-end customer and residential base.

A police car stopped in the middle of the street and an officer watched cautiously as the group—with notebooks in hand, mind you—toured the neighborhood. When they stepped into shops, clerks followed them or asked what they wanted. Customers dining outside returned their greetings with suspicious looks or awkward attempts to clasp their valuables.

Antonio described his feelings after we visited the Grand business district:

> As we started to cross the street, there was this white guy coming the other way. He grabbed for his wallet as if we were going to pick his pockets. Doing that made me feel as if we were not welcome in the neighborhood or we were trying to steal something.

Black kids aren't stupid. They are aware that people, mostly white people, view them through stereotypical lenses. They know when they're not welcome or viewed as threats. On the other hand, they are cognizant that there's a sense of reassurance and pride in their own neighborhoods. Consider these comments from their essays:

> The more we walked, I noticed people looking and wondering what we were doing. We came across this man who asked what we were doing and why. We told him about the things we were doing to make the community a better place. After talking with him, he seemed to change his perspective about the safety of the youth in our community.—Arthur

Keon and Travion describing SPP's mission to a North St. Louis resident

I had a conversation with a resident that impacted me more than anyone I had talked to during the 'Walks.' He shared personal issues about his community. We had small talk, shared a few laughs but, by the end of the conversation, he left me with wisdom and hope. —Travion

***

That simple question of comfort reinforced the power of belonging—that sense of being a part of something that relates to you, your birth, culture and upbringing. If they are connected, students are more receptive to the idea of changing and protecting what belongs to them, their parents, siblings or peers. In their essays, some perfectly spoke to our goals:

We visited the Newstead & Natural Bridge area (northside). This is a neighborhood that can use a lot of work but could also stand on its own. This is a neighborhood that could teach youth like me to use what we have and make the most of it. After all, they made something out of what most people claim to be nothing. —Renesha

The Sweet Potato Project exposed me to things around my

community in ways I have not realized before. Issues I never imagined are now brought to my attention. Not only are we coming together as a group to discuss these problems, we are also making moves to create products and bring wealth back into different black communities. After bringing money into a neighborhood we can invest into things that will benefit surrounding businesses and people.—Travion

***

When They Get it

In our first year of operation the Sweet Potato project in 2012, we ran out of money before the summer session ended. I will never forget the humiliation I felt. It was a Friday, and I told the students that we could no longer pay them their bi-weekly stipends. I stressed that I'd have no hard feelings if they chose not to show up the following week.

On Monday, I was the first to arrive. Not a single student was there. I was heartbroken. Then at 9am on the dot, one student walked around the corner, then two, then another and another. By 9:15, all 15 students showed up. The beautiful thing was they came with ideas: "Mr. Brown let's have a carwash to raise some money; Mr. Brown let's do a dance or a skate party or ..." on and on they went. Priceless!

For me, it was an indication that they got the importance of our program and accepted their roles as change-agents in their communities. I shared the experience with a few professionals who helped me design the program. Their insights helped me appreciate the feeling of belonging to something that's bigger than myself.

"It was about safety," said Tony Neal, educator, consultant and former East St. Louis high school principal.

"It was about belonging, love from the heart as opposed to love from the head...Love from the heart is going the extra mile, staying after the 9-to-5, going to the kid's sporting or extracurricular activities. Doing those extra things, is love from the heart."

"If you look at gangs, it's not much different. You don't get paid for being in the gang, but they show up for activities because there's a sense of safety, belonging and there's some love in that group," Neal explained. He also had an inspiring take on why the students came back to SPP even though we couldn't pay them. "Once they realized that 'hey, wait a minute...I'm in this program'...they understood that they had to show up to get paid. Once they realized that the money had value, they became really concerned about how to keep the program going," Neal said, adding, "But they were willing to stay with or without money. Yes, they wanted the compensation, but they also wanted what they were getting from the adults who were there every day talking to them."

The educator made an interesting point. The students were introduced to speakers who, for the most part, looked like them and showed that they cared about their futures. They were academics, professionals and business-owners. Most came from humble beginnings in neighborhoods our students now call home. These individuals congratulated the students for being a part of our program and expressed confidence in their abilities to create businesses, jobs and economic activity based on the food they grew and the products they can make and sell.

Thankfully, we were able to raise enough money to pay all the kids that summer. But even if we hadn't, the students learned a valuable lesson. A. Bolanle Ambonisye, founder of "Tapping Our Parental Power (TOPP)," a local program that provides information and tools to help improve parent-child relationships, shared another valuable insight:

"They may not be able to see it now, but I'm sure later in life they will point to it as a well-learned lesson, Ambonisye stressed. "They learned about tenacity, delayed gratification and what's really important. And when you think about it, money is a tool—and there are many tools—but what they came for is more important than money."

***

In my reflection about Chef Jeff Henderson's visit to the St. Louis Juvenile Detention Center, I introduced Darria, one of the young female inmates. At Henderson's suggestion, I recruited her into our program in its first year. Darria came to us with an electronic bracelet, the homing device people under house arrest or on probation are required to wear, attached to her ankle. It didn't take long for me to realize the behaviors that had landed her in the center in the first place. Darria had serious problems relating or interacting with her peers. She was loud, impatient and seemed ready for a fight if other students goaded her. Worse yet, she was oftentimes the instigator of disruptive behavior with other students following her lead.

"They learned about tenacity, delayed gratification and what's really important. And when you think about it, money is a tool and there are many tools but what they came for is more important than money."— A. Bolanle Ambonisye

Luckily, I had seen Darria at her best during Henderson's visit. I saw how he empowered her by giving her the role of "leader" among her peers. I decided to try a similar tactic by asking Darria to do me a favor: "The next time the kids are being rude, loud or inconsiderate during a speaker's visit, please loudly and publicly correct their behavior."

She did. We had a speaker and the kids were goofing around. Darria boldly stood up and shouted, "Hey, ya'll being rude! We have a guest, be quiet!" The stunned classmates looked at her, some rolled their eyes, others snickered, but they all did exactly what she told them to do.

After class, Darria came to me. "What just happened?" she asked. I said, "Darria, you have an extraordinary gift but you're not using it correctly. These kids respect you, some fear you. Instead of fighting them, you have the ability to lead them. That's what I want you to do."

For the most part, she did. By giving Darria a role of authority, she belonged, she had a purpose in class. As I mentioned in Chapter Two, because she was diagnosed as bipolar, Darria felt she had been labeled as "stupid." She fought real and imaginary demons to gain respect. Once she was given the responsibility to lead, as she was during Henderson's visit to the detention center, she used her natural skills in a positive manner.

For Darria, it was simply a matter of positive reinforcement: "When adults say positive stuff about me like I'm smart or intelligent, that brings out the positive side of me," she told me.

Two of my daughters attended New City, a private school in midtown St. Louis that uses the multiple intelligences approach developed in 1983 by Dr. Howard Gardner, professor of education at Harvard University. Educators at New City work to find student's areas of strength—be it the arts, music, math, science, etc.—and guide them from their own personal assets. Unfortunately, most overcrowded and underfunded public schools don't have the luxury of focusing on student's individual gifts or strong points. Still, the experience at the school opened my eyes to the positives of alternative educational possibilities.

We've developed a curriculum that's specifically tailored to kids from hard-hit urban areas. By planting produce, learning about sales, marketing, branding, food production and consumer demand, we try to show them how to become entrepreneurs in their own neighborhoods today, not after college graduation.

First, however, we try to combat the years of negativity thrown at them and their neighborhoods. We show them that they do indeed belong, and they can bring valuable contributions to their lives and the lives of others. We know that many at-risk youth are born survivors. They must navigate dangerous terrain daily and learn at early ages to creatively improvise, make a little go a longer way and expertly navigate poverty and public transportation.

I've had many kids in the program like Darria. Most, who were either bullies or distractors, shared Darria's surprise when I urged them to flip their negative attributes and serve as leaders. My students have been challenged to come up with full-blown marketing campaigns that include a product, commercial campaign, branding and costs. I've been amazed at the ideas they come up with in four or so hours.

Urban youth are often judged harshly and unfairly. But they set musical and fashion trends that are appropriated and utilized by mainstream entertainment, fashion and sports entities. Our collective goal should be to tap into their inherent genius and guide them to destinations of greatness. We must not only show them that they are valued, appreciated and needed. We must create environments where they truly understand that they belong.

Growing Up
By Tamera Slater

Growing up has been tough
I've been abandoned so many times I thought there was no love
So bad that I couldn't wait for school time
Only to find out that I'm finna have an even worse mind
See, I got made fun of because I was smart
Like a man that ate beans and had to fart
But that was just the start

I've been to 11 different schools
Thinking that everything back home was all cool
Until I realized that this wasn't right
Waking up every day and having to face a bigger fight
I went through hell, living in a park, being forced to eat chips that were stale
I guess no one knows that I've been from house to house

Some had roaches and one had a mouse

Living with blacks, whites, and Asians

My life so complicated like a quadratic equation

But that was just the start

I thought I got adopted by the right lady

Until her actions became a little shady

Every month she gets a check, but spends it on a new piece of tech

What was it really for?

Because every day I wake up on the floor

I then realized I got to work to stay alive

Like a bunch of bees in a beehive

But even then my life was sore

Because she didn't do anything but take even more

I never had anything, but the man in her life was treated like a king

My mother is unfit and I tried to get her to admit but she only threw a

bigger fit

She picked on me as if I were a scab

Man, my life is such a drag

I guess she didn't really care for me in her heart

But that was just the start

CHAPTER FOUR
When They Are Poor

"I see no changes, wake up in the morning and I ask myself: 'Is life worth living? Should I blast myself?' I'm tired of being poor and, even worse, I'm black My stomach hurts so I'm looking for a purse to snatch..."

—Tupac Shakur, "Changes"

Photo Courtesy of the Sweet Potato Project

Once again, I had missed the message. Over the past seven years, I've had a few kids who always asked that I provide breakfast or snacks throughout the four hours we spend together in class. Whenever a field trip was planned, these students would ask, "Are they feeding us?" To be honest, it got on my nerves. I chided them on occasion: "I pay you guys. It's not the employer's responsibility to feed you, too."

It took me awhile to understand how callous I was. They weren't being greedy or expecting hand-outs. Some were actually hungry! Many attended public schools where the breakfasts and lunches provided are the only nutritious meals they receive throughout the week. "Nutrition" is a foreign word for many of these kids. They get by on salty chips, honeybuns or other fatty, cheap commodities sold at gas stations or neighborhood convenience stores.

It wasn't until other students or SPP volunteers told me about some of the students living conditions that I came to fully realize the impact that poverty and hunger had on them. Today, I'm a bit more empathetic. If we can afford it, I try to bring snacks in the morning or I buy them something to eat during our "Neighborhood Walks."

I really should have known better. I was born and raised in poverty. My siblings and I were hungry often. My impoverished upbringing served as my guide when I tried to articulate the realities of poverty to my readers. As the executive director of an entrepreneurial program for youth, I was preaching independence to students who really had no basic sustenance.

I had forgotten "the walk."

In 2004, as a columnist for the *St. Louis Post-Dispatch*, I set out to understand the environment of students the newspaper had lambasted over a series of fights at Vashon High School on the city's North side. The school is in a low-income part of North St. Louis. I wondered what images the kids confronted on their daily trek to school. In looking for answers to the reportedly disruptive behavior, I took a three-block walk to Vashon.

I started at Cass and Jefferson avenues, the sight of the now demolished Pruitt-Igoe Housing complex and walked west to the school. The first business I noticed was Flamingo Package Liquor. There was a rent-by-the-hour motel and a nightclub connected to the place. A banner outside the club promoted "Kools" and Newport cigarettes. Another touted the "irresistibly different" taste of a cognac beverage called "HPNOTIQ."

A few feet further, kids passed a block-long junk yard of rusted, dead cars gutted for workable parts. The blocks in front, on the side and behind Vashon all offer varying versions of destruction. Slum properties, liquor stores, trash-filled lots, burned-out or abandoned buildings abounded. It couldn't possibly be an inspirational walk for the students, I thought. The Third World environment seemed out of context with desired academic outcomes.

The walk took me about 25 minutes. Along the way, I imagined being mugged, attacked by stray dogs or bonked on the head from falling bricks. I also noticed how easy it was to pull a child into an abandoned building or empty tractor trailer.

I arrived at my car feeling tense, my senses were on alert. I placed a fat foot on the gas pedal to speed away. Looking in the rearview mirror, I looked at the beautiful $40 million school surrounded by poverty and deprivation. The image stayed with me as I drove away.

But "driving away," is a luxury most poor, public school kids don't have.

***

According to the Census Bureau, more than 364,000 Missourians (6.2 percent) live in deep poverty—meaning they live below the poverty line which, in 2016, was $24,563 for a family of four. For African Americans in Missouri, 24.8 percent live below the poverty rate. While whites still constitute the largest single group of Americans living in poverty, American Indians and Alaskan Native (28.4 percent), African-Americans (27.4 percent) and Hispanics (26.6 percent) are still disproportionately overrepresented.

For minority children, the statistics are grimmer. The poverty rate for Black children was 38.2 percent; 32.3 percent for Hispanic children;

17 percent for non-Hispanic White children; and 13 percent for Asian children, based on U.S. Census data in 2010. The economy has improved within the past few years. Therefore, the poverty rate has also improved. But, as it often does, when the economic pendulum sways in the opposite direction, the poor and dispossessed disproportionately suffer the greatest impact.

The students I've taught don't acknowledge or complain about poverty. I suppose things haven't changed that much over the years. I knew my family was poor but so was everyone else in our neighborhoods, I thought. Tamika was a student that had been with me for about three years. One day, I dropped her and some of the other students off after class. I took Tamika to one location where she knocked on a door with no answer. She climbed back into the van and directed me to another location, then another. No one opened the doors. She told me to leave her at the last residence because someone was expected home soon. I did.

One of her close friends lamented about Tamika's plight as we drove away. "I hope she'll be OK. She's been living from place-to-place for years now." I came to find out that Tamika was a product of the foster home system. She had been bounced from home-to-home since she was a grade-schooler. The three addresses I took her were homes of relatives or former foster parents. Tamika had no permanent residence at the time. She was a senior at the top of the school's achievement list and she played at least four musical instruments.

> *"Tamika was a product of the foster home system. She had been bounced from home-to-home since she was a grade-schooler."*

Because of this young lady, I looked at the numbers of homeless young people with deeper introspection. The United States Conference of Mayors reported that, in 2010, more than 1.6 million children (1 in 45) in America were homeless. According to the report, approximately 650,000 are below age 6. Although black children make up only 15 percent of the U.S. child population, approximately 47 percent of the children in homeless families are black.

Tamika was also one of the kids who always asked me about food or snacks. She speaks with determination about becoming a nurse and an entrepreneur. She had a child after graduating high school that she dotes on with the love and attention she *hadn't* received growing up.

She is but one of my students who've inspired and humbled me as they quietly and defiantly grapple with desperate poverty. They are the current-day reflection of a people, like their ancestors, who deal with generational adversities without griping or giving up. Tamika has her eye on "the prize," with very little economic, social or parental reinforcement. Students like Tamika may be too prideful to articulate the perils of poverty. Therefore, those of us concerned about their health, happiness and futures must serve as their voice and be the instigators of holistic change.

***

It's Hard to Learn When You're Hungry

As a kid, I was not aware that poverty was one of the reasons I did poorly in school or dropped out in my sophomore year. Although I acknowledge the inherent ability of black folk to make lemonade out of lemons, we must do better as a society to address hunger and poverty, especially among disproportionately impacted minority youth.

According to psychological research, poverty impacts a child's physical and mental health and other factors that affect their outcomes in school, neighborhoods or in the workplace. Substandard housing, homelessness, inadequate nutrition and food insecurity, insufficient child care, limited-to-no healthcare access, and unsafe neighborhoods are all linked to adverse poverty. According to the American Psychological Association, poorer children and teens are also at greater risk for poor academic achievement, school dropout, abuse and neglect, behavioral and socio-emotional problems, physical health problems and developmental delays.

Chronic stress associated with living in poverty adversely impacts a child's learning ability. The National Center for Education reported that the dropout rate of students living in low-income families is about four and one-half times greater than the rate of children from higher-income-earning families. Additionally, children living in poverty are at greater risk of behavioral and emotional problems; including impulsiveness, difficulty getting along with peers, aggression, attention deficit disorders (ADHD) and conduct disorder.

The SPP Approach

"America has the opportunity to help bridge the gap between the haves and the have-nots. The question is, will it do it or not."—Dr. Martin Luther King, Jr., March 1968

According to the RWJF Health & Society Scholars Program study, "Black-White Differences in Avoidable Mortality in the United States," death from preventable or treatable conditions account for nearly 70 percent of the black-white mortality difference. The study found that blacks die disproportionately from treatable illnesses such as stroke, hypertension, diabetes, colon cancer, appendicitis and even the flu.

Poor kids live in environments where access to affordable health care is a matter of having good jobs and salaries. It's where poor eating habits are directly linked to slave plantations and where getting healthy, nutritious food may mean a car-ride miles away from their homes. Getting these kids to understand and address healthy living and eating is a major challenge. My students come from neighborhoods where fatty and sugary foods serve as their daily sustenance and where there are few parks for play and exercise, which fuels childhood obesity. Many also live where they've been routinely exposed to environmental contaminants like lead paint or toxic waste dumps. Therefore, they suffer from disproportionate chronic conditions such as asthma, anemia and pneumonia. Advertisings near their homes promote irresponsible behaviors like smoking, drinking alcohol or engaging in sexual activity. We also can't underestimate their exposure to violence within their communities, which can lead to trauma, injury, disability and low mortality rates.

Sadly, at-risk children grow accustomed to at-risk behaviors. Talking about ways to improve their health is like speaking a foreign language. One thing my students *do* understand is money. They know its role in getting the things they want in life. With this in mind, we seek to monetarily incentivize healthy eating. They grow food and make food-based products, which means they are taught to sell their goods to consumers. Therefore, they must understand and explain why their food is a better alternative for their parents, peers and customers. They know that sweet potatoes are an excellent source of *vitamins A, C, B1* and *B2* and a good source of *potassium* and *dietary fiber*. They know that the sweet potato cookies they make are lower in fat and sugar than popular store-bought cookies.

"Sadly, at-risk children grow accustomed to at-risk behaviors. Talking about ways to improve their health is like speaking a foreign language. One thing my students do understand is money. They know its role in getting the things they want in life."

We're not naïve. We know that growing and selling healthy food will not change engrained habits, lack of money or the environmental contaminants that contribute to poor health. Therefore, we encourage our students to imagine themselves as young, urban pioneers on a mission to recreate and revitalize disadvantaged neighborhoods. Yes, food is the starting place, but we also preach land-ownership and entrepreneurism. We want to help foster a generation of change-agents.

We also understand that youth cannot carry out the larger mission of neighborhood revitalization on their own. We will also need adult land-owners and food-growers. Politicians are needed to draft legislation for urban advancement like they do for well-to-do developers. I would like to see a food manufacturing plant in North St. Louis. Industrialization may be a thing of the past for urban areas, but everybody eats. We see food as a viable way to grow small businesses, create jobs, serve restaurants, bakeries, grocers and consumers locally, regionally and nationally.

Poverty is the number one factor that fuels crime, malnutrition, low birth-rates, poor educational outcomes, health maladies and death at early ages. We at SPP are of the belief that there is no silver bullet or magic remedy that will solve the historic and disproportionate challenges poor children and neighborhoods of color face. The only answer, as far as I'm concerned, is to foster and support a collective "do-for-self" attitude in low income communities. Food and the money it can generate is a sound way to incentivize vibrant, sustainable change.

The young people we've mentored are ready to play their part. I'm not sure the same can be said about adults. However, I remain hopeful that more and more of us adults will face the bigger challenge of helping young people lead fruitful, productive, healthier and more economically stable lives. Not only for themselves and their neighborhoods, but for all of us.

CHAPTER FIVE
When They are Traumatized

> *"People need to take into consideration that hip-hop traditionally has always been a reflection of the environment. If you want to change the content of the music, change the environment of the artist."*

—Rapper T.I. on The Daily Show with Trevor Noah/Sept. 15, 2016

Myke King / Photo by Benjamin Gandhi-Shepard

The students and I referred to them as "The Dread Brothers." They varied in size and hue, but each adorned manes of thick dreadlocks. From what I gathered, the brothers had different fathers and lived together off and on throughout their lives. But they were tight. At the time, 2014, they were sometimes goofy, but they rose to the challenges we presented them. Travion, 19 at the time, was the most serious. He earned praise from our instructors and the business-owners we visited that summer. He was an inquisitive kid who asked probing, deep questions. Yet he told me that the educators and adults in his life had never praised him for his wit. My heart dropped the day he said, "Mr. Brown, you're the first person to tell me I'm smart."

About the third week of classes that year, The Dread Brothers started acting rather weird. They were too playful, too distracted and sometimes too disruptive. One day, one of our instructors, Muhammad Raqib, called the brothers out on their behavior.

"Mr. Raqib, you don't know what we're going through!" the middle brother, Antonio, shot back. Raqib insisted he elaborate. He did. Antonio told the class how he and his brothers attended a party that weekend. During the festivities, their uncle's throat was slashed by a female acquaintance. Antonio spoke of the helplessness he felt as he applied a towel to the ghastly wound to no avail. The brother's beloved uncle passed away.

The incident was a graphic example of what urban youth often grapple with every day. We read or see news headlines about cases of murder or violent crime in their neighborhoods. More often than not, most of us judge and condemn young people. We scratch our collective heads believing that black youth "choose" violence. Conservative pundits, like Bill O'Reilly, blame hip-hop, failed parenting, failed communities and cultural deficiencies, to underscore a racist and narrow-minded belief that poor, black kids and black families are devoid of "family values."

Rarely do we consider that these youth routinely navigate death, poverty, gangs and drug-related violence. What complicates the problem with many is their inability to articulate their pain, loss or fear from acts of violence.

SPP student, Keith Young

Consider, Keith, a 19-year-old student of the 2013 Sweet Potato Project class. In an interview for *Youth & The City*, a podcast created by a local architect, Jasmine Aber, Keith recalled a harrowing event: "The other day, I was walking in my neighborhood and some dude, one of the Bloods, I think, started asking me questions like, 'where you from,' 'what you doing around here?' I kept walking thinking, 'don't trip, don't trip.' He was like, 'I don't want to see you around here no more.' Then he showed me his gun. I didn't know if he was gonna shoot or what. It made me so mad. I kept thinking, 'man, I need a gun.' There's always drama like that going on."

There is, indeed, routine "drama" in low-income neighborhoods. One thing that stays with me, though, is how non-plussed my students seem when they recount the incidences of the violence they encounter. It's as if dealing with the "drama" is a normal part of growing up poor and black.

Take for instance an incident in 2012. I had driven Darryeon Bishop, one of my senior students, home after class. Before enrolling in college at Southeast Missouri State University, Darryeon lived in a high-crime area of North St. Louis near the water tower on Grand Blvd. There was a discarded car bumper, broken glass and bits and pieces of car parts scattered in the street not far from the front door of the 4-unit building Darryeon's family occupied.

"Wow, looks like someone had a pretty bad accident," I commented.

"That was no accident, Mr. Brown," Darryeon responded, far too nonchalantly for my taste. "That was a drive-by."

This wasn't the only act of violence Darryeon had witnessed. One day he told me that he'd seen a man shot in broad daylight. He'd watched the man breathe his last breath, bleeding on the side of his car. It was the casual way Darryeon shared the story that disturbed me.

For centuries, African Americans have conditioned themselves and their offspring to be tough, be quiet and just accept what society throws at them. It may be a self-preservation mechanism, but it has resulted in dangerous psychological conditioning where young people are encouraged to keep their fears bottled-up until it explodes in a variety of unforeseen ways.

Society cavalierly labels low-income neighborhoods as "combat zones." Yet, the term Post-Traumatic Stress Disorder, or PTSD, is reserved for war veterans. Growing research, however, suggests that children living in violent environments are indeed suffering from PTSD.

Howard Spivak M.D., director of the U.S. Centers for Disease Control and Division of Violence Prevention said; "Youth living in inner cities show a higher prevalence of post-traumatic stress disorder than soldiers." Spivak's research, which was included in a 2012 congressional briefing, illustrates how many inner-city children essentially live in "combat zones." Unlike soldiers, however, kids like

Keith and Darryeon never leave the "war zone" and are oftentimes victims of repetitious trauma.

According to the U.S. Department of Justice's 2008 National Survey of Children's Exposure to Violence, more than 60 percent of children in this country have been exposed to violence, either as witnesses or by learning about incidences of violence from family members or friends. Although the numbers may seem shockingly high, it resonates in the experiences I've had with our students. A few have hard edges, and I've come to learn why. At young ages, some have lived lives that make my childhood look like playtime in the Hamptons.

Let me give you a couple examples from 2013:

One of my students, Frederick, lost his brother to violence during our summer session. Another, Charnell, told us about her brother who was brutally assassinated, "gangland style," two years earlier. Nadia said she saw folks shot near her front lawn in North St. Louis. During one of our morning news sessions, I asked the 2017 class to raise their hands if they've lost a friend, relative or loved one to violence.

At least 15 out of 20 hands stretched toward the ceiling.

Under-funded, under-staffed and overwhelmed public schools aren't equipped to effectively deal with the traumatization of poor, minority kids. The societal remedy most often provided is juvenile and, later, adult detention. We systematically lock these kids up, lock them out, and dismiss and demean them based on undiagnosed stimuli from their neighborhoods.

"When children of color act up, we don't try to get to the meat of what's affecting that child. Instead, we adjudicate them and move them through the system," says Lanada Williams, a psychotherapist and CEO of Alliance Family Solutions, a private counseling practice in Washington DC.

In a Dec. 2014 interview with ThinkProgress, a news site dedicated to providing "progressive" information, Williams said: "People don't realize those experiences affect children psychologically. Evidence of this might be when a child does not want to walk down particular streets. Another externalizing behavior is acting out and being destructive in school, often cursing out teachers and bullying others."

"When children of color act up, we don't try to get to the meat of what's affecting that child."—Lanada Williams, CEO of Alliance Family Solutions

A March 4, 2014 article written by Michelle Chen for America. aljazeera.com explored "the PTSD epidemic in mostly violent neighborhoods." The article should have been a clarion call for the American educational system to confront the effects of community violence and psychological trauma that plague children of color. Chen stated that "the combat metaphors range from children caught in the crossfire to explosions of gang warfare to SWAT-like police teams patrolling the streets. But behind the bleak imagery lies the hidden collateral damage of people's tender psychological wounds. It's an epidemic of trauma-related stress in the hospitals, schools and living rooms of these beleaguered communities."

The Centers for Disease Control's 2016 study found that 2/3rds of the general population are affected by childhood trauma and toxic stress. The CDC's "Adverse Childhood Experience" study looked at how hostile childhood experiences such as abuse, neglect, and violence are linked to chronic health conditions, low-life potential and early death.

"But behind the bleak imagery lies the hidden collateral damage of people's tender psychological wounds."

During a Feb. 2017 *St. Louis on the Air* interview, Emily Luft, program director of Alive & Well STL, an initiative of the St. Louis Regional Health Commission, described how toxic stress impacts children biologically: "The things in our life like poverty, living in violent communities, not knowing where your next meal is going to come from…in our body, that triggers the same physiological reaction as if a bear entered the studio right now."

Public school teachers aren't equipped to handle 20 or so "bears" in classrooms with 30 are more students. The task is even harder when we aren't zoned into the conditions that impact their behavior. Or, like in my classroom case, when I misread the signs and assumed The Dread Brothers were just acting out for no reason. The challenge, I believe, is creating safe spaces where our youth can unpack, unload, share and understand that they are not alone in the chaos.

***

"A Moment to Vent"

Muhammad Raqib conducting a SPP class

I will be forever grateful for Muhammad Raqib. In 2014, while pursuing his master's degree, he was also a part-time instructor for our program. Raqib was skilled enough to see the cue when one of the Dread Brothers said, "You don't know what we're going through!"

"I felt they needed a moment to vent, a moment of clarity, a moment to spill their guts and tell it like it is," Raqib told me after class. "Those young guys were angry, they were mad. They had to tell their story. Sharing that incident created a new kind of bond in the class. It seemed like the whole room dealt with the story as if they all knew the victim. Maybe in a sense, they did."

The curriculum of the first two weeks of the Sweet Potato Project is dedicated to communication. In group dynamics, we've found that the students are sometimes loud, interactive and playfully engaged. Yet, many are hesitant to talk about their lives or experiences in front of the class. We've created several activities to get them to open up. One of the first things we do is have them interview one another. The interviewee tells the class about the student: what part of the city they're from, their family background, their dreams and aspirations, etc.

Secondly, as I mentioned earlier, we start every morning with a review of the news. At first, I found it disturbing that most of the students gravitated toward stories of violence or crime. But, after a while, I noticed how those stories ignited personal reflections of murders or death in their lives. A story about a neighborhood drive-by, for instance, elicited personal reflections about similar incidences or the frustration they held about violence in their neighborhoods.

"Those young guys were angry, they were mad. They had to tell their story.
—Muhammad Raqib

The news round-up serves as a means to keep kids informed about things in and outside their bubbles, but it's also become a form of group therapy. A way to get them to, as Raqib noted, "vent."

"My two brothers were murdered," Raqib told the class. "One was 14 years-old when he had his face blown off. The other was 23 and was shot five times by someone he knew. I had to talk about that because the pain and anger was setting in. I had to process that. It wasn't until I started talking in groups, taking workshops on motivational speaking, that I started to get better, that I started to heal, to process and understand that life happens to all of us."

Group therapy, Raqib insists, should be a part of every public-school's agenda, especially those in high-crime neighborhoods. He's not calling for anything revolutionary, just something akin to programs like Alcoholics Anonymous. "We need something that's oriented to acknowledge the pain in a group setting while stressing one's ability to overcome or reconcile challenging circumstances," Raqib says.

Ongoing trauma and grief counseling sessions became a necessity after a 20-year-old gunman shot 20 children between the ages of six and seven, as well as six adults, in 2012 at Sandy Hook Elementary School in Newton, Connecticut. A group of teachers secured grants to fund ongoing trauma and grief counseling for students directly affected by the incident. The shooting took place in a quiet, upper/middle class suburb. Although the incident sparked national conversations about gun violence and childhood mental health, it didn't lead to nationwide action to address the violence that impacts low-income neighborhoods and students across the country. Kids in these neighborhoods also need ongoing therapy to address endless trauma, Raqib stressed.

Tyrone C. Howard, associate dean for equity and inclusion at UCLA, seems to agree. "Schools can do a better job of talking about the extent to which student trauma exists, teaching children coping mechanisms, and providing mental-health services," Howard said.

The New Visions Charter High School for Advanced Math and Science in the Bronx offers another innovative approach. Hip-hop therapy has become part of the culture at the school, where most of the students are black or Latino. The after-school club was started in 2014 by Ian P. Levy, a school counselor determined to develop a therapy model as part of his doctoral research.

"When traumatic events happen, it's important that students have a space to digest them," Levy told a *New York Times'* reporter.

With funds raised through a crowdfunding site, Levy bought about $3,000 worth of recording equipment. Students write and record songs in a corner of his office. They rap about violence, suicides, police shootings and other negative contributors. One student, Ellis McBeth, became angry after the death of his 12-year-old cousin. Before hip-hop therapy, McBeth said he picked fights with other students and used aggression to express his feelings. After his cousin's death, he wrote a song and had his older sister sing the bridge:

"I want to say R.I.P. to you because I don't believe it's true, but I'll still remember you."

"When traumatic events happen, it's important that students have a space to digest them." —Ian P. Levy of New Visions School

In an interview with the *New York Times*, McBeth explained how he transitioned from a kid who would "throw a punch" to suppress inside feelings, to a burgeoning artist who combats negative feelings with music: "Now I make songs about them. I write verses that cool me down."

***

Educators at Sandy Hook, New Visions and other progressive schools have found ways to raise money to address the trauma young people constantly face. There's a plethora of research that justifies federal, state and local resources aimed at addressing the mental ravages of violence and youth trauma. A local politician, State Rep. Bruce Franks Jr. (D-St. Louis), may be leading the charge in drafting legislation that will help under-funded school districts with this problem.

In mid-2018, Frank's bill, HCR70, declaring youth violence "a public health epidemic" was signed into law. The bill calls for the reinforcement of statewide trauma-informed education, which would assist in enhancing awareness and understanding regarding the topic of trauma-informed approaches and trauma-specific interventions for teachers and students.

Franks is no stranger to trauma. As a child, his younger brother, Christopher, was used as a human shield in a gun fight and lost his life. Part of Frank's bill declares June 7th "Christopher Harris Day" in the state of Missouri. In drafting the resolution, Franks noted that it's important that the state create "avenues for increased resources" for trauma-informed education. "The underlying causes of trauma include but don't exclude undiagnosed mental health issues, quality of living conditions, poverty, parental instability, exposure to violence in families and communities and many more aspects of our everyday life," Franks says.

The importance of Franks' bill is that it quantifies youth violence as a public health issue. This, he says, will help direct resources to the root cause of the epidemic and the long-term impact violence and trauma have on young people's psyches. "We have to remember that conditions will often lead individuals to believe that injustices are just," Franks said. "Young people have become so accustomed to violence in their communities that they feel as though there are no other options, which in some cases is very true."

In the seven years since starting SPP, I've learned a lot from our students. I've had clashes with some who thought they had no other way—other than a violent, emotive or aggressive way—to express themselves. We're adapting, trying to add more social services experts and innovative, informed ways to help them express themselves productively.

Programs that attempt to work with this demographic must be empathetic, strategic and reality-based. Raqib reminds us that disadvantaged youth suffer greatly from trauma not of their making. It's not a phantom ailment. It's real and in need of comprehensive remedies to help at-risk youth heal and deal with life.

"Before they can become entrepreneurs, they have to deal with their mess," Raqib told me. "They must deal with the emotional, physical, psychological mess that they're in to become constructive entrepreneurs. If they don't talk about it and get it out, it will destroy whatever it is they have going on or whatever it is they want to accomplish in life."

REFLECTION

The Deal

Originally published Sept. 12, 2013

http://sylvesterbrownjr.blogspot.com/

Photo Courtesy of the Sweet Potato Project

There I was, working in the food pantry of St. Elizabeth Mother of John the Baptist Catholic Church. At my side that day was an 18-year-old preparing boxes for the needy. A 19-year-old student was with me the next day. Both teens were part of the Sweet Potato Project. We were making amends for a transgression; paying a penance, trying to regain trust.

It was, after all, part of our deal.

It all started on the last day of our summer session. Excitement was in the air. It was payday. The good times came to a crashing halt when I learned that three of my boys who had been asked to help in the church's food pantry were accused of stealing a volunteer's cell phone.

I was livid. The church had allowed us to conduct classes that summer at its affiliate school, St. Louis Catholic Academy. The supportive staff had become loving mentors and had nothing but compliments about our youth—until that fateful day.

"How dare you jeopardize this program," I yelled at the three boys. "After all we've learned about dignity, responsibility and self-respect... how dare you damage the reputation of this program and your fellow students?"

The rock-headed teens formed an alliance. No one would indict the other or admit they had stolen the phone. Nor did any indicate they would return it. Not at first anyway.

The other students were paid and dismissed. The three teens had to stay behind to face the wrath of myself; Herman Noah, board member with the North Area Community Development Corporation; our fiscal agency and Tallis Piaget, a local author and dedicated volunteer that summer. Those boys weren't leaving the room until the phone was returned.

Eventually, after a good dressing down, one of the boys fessed up. The phone was retrieved and returned to the elderly volunteer.

"Why did you steal the phone?" I asked the culprit who will remain anonymous.

"Because it was red," he stupidly answered. This kid was a member of the "Bloods." He'd been in the gang since elementary school. In some twisted way, he was still captivated by the gang's color—red.

The boys were sent home without pay. I told them that I needed to talk with Mr. Noah and Tallis about their punishment. I also needed to reflect on the advice some my students who started with the program last year had given me. Barry and Myke, in particular, had accused me of being too soft, too lax with some of the rowdier students. I should "fire them," they repeatedly insisted.

Their point was well taken but I challenged them. "Listen guys, we have a group of students this year from some of the poorest, most crime-filled neighborhoods in the city. They're used to being suspended, shut out, kicked out or fired from something. I want this program to be different. I want us to find a way to turn the worse kids around and I need your help doing it."

It's a huge mandate for young people but the Sweet Potato Project is unlike traditional public or charter schools' programs. We want the knuckleheads and the hard-to-reach. We're dedicated to creating a generation of urban entrepreneurs. And, if we are serious about creating jobs and businesses in the North St. Louis, we're going to have to find ways to empower the dismissed and discarded. Some are beyond rescue, but I maintain that we must create avenues of redemption for those willing to step up to the challenge.

After reflections and discussions, I contacted the three boys. "Since you all took part in this theft, you all must pay restitution," I said. I offered them a deal. If they went back to the food pantry, humbled themselves and faced their accusers and worked two days for free, I'd give them their last paycheck and allow them back into the program.

Two of the boys showed up on different days. When I accompanied the first to the pantry, a senior volunteer said she didn't trust him and didn't want him in the facility. This was understandable. However, the elderly volunteer who had her phone stolen disagreed with that decision. She allowed the boy to work under her supervision. I still marvel at her gentle, but stern, grandmotherly advice as she put the boy to work. "He's a good kid and a hard worker," she assured me at the end of the day. "I just hope you've learned something today," she told my student.

She wasn't there when I returned with the other student, the one who actually stole the phone, but he told me she had called him. She had forgiven him for his deed and gave him the same advice she'd given his partner. As we walked home after working that day, I continued the lecture. "You have leadership ability, young man. After all, you convinced a group of gullible young men to cover for your crime. Unfortunately, you have a gift that you're using for evil." I then added, "If you let me, I'll show how to turn your weaknesses into strengths."

He said he'd try. Parting, I could only hope he and his wayward cohorts would learn something from the incident. There's a way to reclaim dignity and the trust of others if you man-up after you mess up.

He is but one of the kids I've written about that give me great concern. They're not in school, have no jobs and they are prone to dangerous distractions. I'm frustrated that we still haven't raised enough money to resume classes and get them working a couple days a week maintaining the sweet potato lots. It's not a lot of money but at least I can give them something while keeping my eyes on them and hopefully inspiring them. We reached out to these kids and welcomed the chaos that comes with their environments. We've sparked their imaginations. I've told them that they will be the urban pioneers who will show the city that we can indeed plant produce and create products from North St. Louis.

A promise is a promise. I'm not giving up on them. I can't.

After all, we made a deal.

Entrepreneur Alex Carlson helps students Plant at Botanical Gardens

Student Barry Goins practicing piano Photo by Benjamin Gandhi-Shepard

SPP Students planting on vacant lot

Photographer, Benjamin Gandhi-Shepard with students

Student Marquitta with me during photo shoot for Aetna Calendar

Bolanle Ambonisye's Conflict Resolution class

Student, Charles Hill

Charnell Hurn /Harvesting 2012 Photo by Benjamin Gandhi-Shepard

Chef Steve Jenkins preparing students to make sweet potato cookies at St. Louis University

Elesha and Marquitta Photo by Benjamin Gandhi-Shepard

Student, Andivar Allen

Class on police interaction at William J. Harrison Center

Student, Darryeon Bishop selling cookies / Winter 2013

Tytianna, Renesha and Keyundra / Neighborhood Walk / 2014

Briana and Mirramoni / 2013 harvest

Planting sweet potatoes on vacant lot / 2013

Students during Neighborhood Walk on Grand Business District

Student Essay Reading / Photo by Benjamin Gandhi-Shepard

Student interview exercise 2013

Nadia Epps by Benjamin Gandhi-Shepard

Keon and Charnell / First harvest 2012

Chef Bryan helping students bake at St. Louis University

Interview with documentarian, Ruella Rouf

Planting at Union Ave. Church lot

Students with Alex Carlson, owner of Red Guitar Bread

Architecture design class at Creative Exchange Laboratory

Planting on vacant lot / 2012

Students learning the hauling and demolition trades

Dashia Martin watering beds

Class with artist/entrepreneur, Cbabi Bayoc

Architecture class at Creative Exchange Laboratory (CEL)

Packaged sweet potato cookies

Students at Scholarship
training center

First cookie-baking session
2012

"Mad City Money" financial literacy class with UMSL
Pro. Grant C. Black

Visiting neighborhood fire department
2016

North St. Louis Neighborhood
Walk / 2014

Packaging cookies at
St. Louis University

Students planting sweet potatoes
on huge vacant lot

Students with owner of MoKabe's Coffee shop

Antonio and Travion with sweet potato brownies

Students at Rise Coffee Shop in
the Grove area

SLU's Chef Steve Jenkins
making cookies

With James Forbes of
Good Life Growing, LLC

Students at Ranken
Technical College in midtown St. Louis

Planting at Good Life Growing's
"Old Orchid" Urban Farm

Owners of SWAA Cleaning
Services

Neighborhood Walk in
North St. Louis

At La Vallesana on the
Cherokee Strip

Land-ownership class with
SLU Prof. Dr. Patricia Lee

Computer lab at William J. Harrison
learning Center

With Jason Wilson owner of
Chronicle Coffee

Student's presentation at Afro
World Hair & Fashion

Promoting SPP Blues Fundraiser
with Marquis Knox

With Nicole Adewala of Abna
Construction

With St. Louis Police Lt. Col.
Ronnie Robinson

Me planting with students at Union
Ave Church lot

Students and I planting at Old Orchid lot

With author and motivational speaker,
Koran Bolden

First cookie recipe with
Reine Bayoc

Lewis Reed, President of the St.
Louis Board of Aldermen

Volunteer and artist
Robert Powell

Planting at the Missouri   Students at Harvest Café   Businessman, Kabir Muhammad
Botanical Garden

Fundraiser at the Royale Restaurant   Students with SLU Chef, Bryan Rogers

SPP Cookie label   Class with St. Louis health   Putting organic soil in
                        department   beds on vacant lot

Students visit Scooters Candy store in   Paul Miller / Photo by Benjamin Gandhi-Shepard
North St. Louis

With author and airline pilot,
Gerald Higginbotham

Students with Mike Brown,
Sr., father of Mike Brown

With architect and owner of CEL, Jasmin Aber

Students at Ranken Technical School

Students with Sterling Moody,
owner of Supreme Carwash

Students at Union Ave. Church lot / 2016

Tyler Matthew's Business Plan class

CHAPTER SIX
When They Are Validated

"And these children that you spit on as they try to change their worlds are immune to your consultations, they're quite aware of what they're going through."

—David Bowie, "Changes"

Photo by Richard Reilly

As I started writing this chapter, thousands of young people were in America's streets demanding gun control legislation. Seventeen people were killed and seventeen more wounded on February 14, 2018, at *Marjory Stoneman Douglas High School* in Parkland, Florida. The 19-year-old suspect, Nikolas Cruz, used a legally-purchased AR-15-style rifle to carry out the mass shooting. The incident prompted youth to publicly call for stricter gun control laws.

On a gut level, we all know guns are a problem in this country.

According to the CDC, 87 percent of all homicides against people of all age groups were committed with firearms. Sixteen percent of deaths among people age 15 to 24 are due to homicide. We also know that gun violence is more common in urban and poor communities. Again, according to the CDC, of all black males murdered between the ages of 15 and 24, a majority — 54 percent — were killed with a gun.

David Hogg, a senior at the *Stoneman Douglas,* was one of the first of many students making public demands for stricter gun laws. "We're children. You guys are the adults," Hogg said. "You need to take some action and play a role. Work together. [Get] over your politics and get something done!"

There is no sadder example of adults failing to listen to young people than the callous reactions to their remonstrations. Instead of proactively responding to the kids—some of which were actual victims of the shooting—many right-leaning pundits criticized and chastised them.

"They're being led by "left wing gun control activists," said Jack Kingston, a CNN contributor and former U.S. Representative from Georgia. Kingston claimed the students' grief was possibly "hijacked by left-wing groups who have an agenda."

In other right-wing corridors, talking heads like Rush Limbaugh, Alex Jones (Info Wars) and former Fox News host Bill O'Reilly portrayed the protestors as "crisis actors," pawns of the Democrat Party and gun control activists, "anti-Trump kids," FBI plants or co-conspirators intent on exploiting the tragedy just to undermine our 2nd Amendment rights. In my city, popular, conservative commentator Jamie Allman's sick March 26th Tweet of "...getting ready to ram a hot poker up David Hogg's ass..." cost him his radio and TV gigs.

All this ugly rhetoric because young people comprising the

"March for Our Lives" movement had the gumption to challenge the all-powerful National Rifle Association (NRA) and the politicians it supports through its army of lobbyists and immense political donations.

In an NBCNEWS commentary, actor, director and educator LeVar Burton opined that youth, unlike many adults, realize the country is indeed in deep trouble. "When we're willing to sacrifice our children on the altar of guns and a special interest lobby, we've sold our souls, and that's the truth. We have sold our souls, and these kids aren't having it," Burton wrote.

"When we're willing to sacrifice our children on the altar of guns and a special interest lobby, we've sold our souls, and that's the truth. We have sold our souls, and these kids aren't having it."—Levar Burton

The former Star Trek star makes a valid point. Despite the ignorant political pomposity, young protestors are determined to move the needle on the national discussion of gun safety reform. What's more, by sheer numbers alone, a chill must creep up and down the spines of obliging politicians who realize that right now or very soon, millions of articulate, media-savvy young people will have the power to vote them out of office.

Though they were assailed, the young protestors were also validated. Their public actions were recognized and, as a result, were intensified by positive mainstream press and public affirmation. Because of this validation, hordes of young activists will no doubt be a force of political reckoning now and in the very near future.

The challenge, as I see it, is not to create more protestors, even though that's not a bad thing. It's to find communal ways to validate the creativity, resiliency and righteous anger of not just the "March for Our Lives" protestors but all young people who have the audacity to confront stale, restricted thinking and blaze a progressive path of their own making.

***

In a country still marred by race, I would be remiss not to point out the different reactions to the majority white kids profiled after the Parkland shooting vs youngsters involved with the Black Lives Matter (BLM) protests. In a bizarre interview with Moonie Times, newly elected NRA president and retired Marine lieutenant colonel Oliver North tried to paint a familiar canvas when attempting to define the Stoneman Douglas protesters: "They call them activists...they're not activists — this is civil terrorism," North said. "This is the kind of thing that's never been seen against a civil rights organization in America. You go back to the terrible days of Jim Crow and those kinds of things ...we didn't have the cyberwar kind of thing that we've got today."

North's description didn't catch on outside his loyal gun-toting base. Try as they might, pundits were no match against televised images of mostly suburban, mostly white kids standing up for their lives and safety in schools. However, with stereotypes at the ready, those same voices criminalized black protestors to the point where a petition was put forth asking the government to label BLM a "terrorist" organization. The petition garnered more than 141,000 signatures.

But, as Burton noted, the March for Our Lives students weren't "having it." During the March 24th national protests, the students repeatedly spoke of their "white privilege" and the media's failure to give "black students a voice."

"My school is about 25 percent black, but the way we're covered doesn't reflect that," Hogg said during a speech the Friday before a planned weekend of national marches.

Jaclyn Corin, a survivor of the shooting, added, "We recognize that Parkland received more attention because of its affluence…but we share this stage today and forever with those communities who have always stared down the barrel of a gun."

The young people who routinely face gun violence—be it on ghetto streets or at the hands of biased police—have been ignored, marginalized and mischaracterized during national protests and demonstrations in the wake of Mike Brown's death in August of 2014.

Still, there are hopeful signs that an activated and engaged young voter-base can indeed change the trajectory of our nation. According to an analysis conducted by the Harvard Institute of Politics (IOP), voters between the ages of 18 and 29 "were absolutely crucial" to the Democratic takeover of the House of Representatives during the 2018 midterm elections.

Per the IOP analysis, 31 percent of voters under 30 voted in the 2018 election, representing 13 percent of the total electorate. By comparison, young voters represented 10 percent in the 2014 midterm national electorate. This is far below the estimated 51 percent of eligible millennial voters in the 2016 presidential election but it's an impressive turnout for a midterm election. It definitely means young voters played a key role in the 2018 historic high voter turnout. It also means they helped send a record number of diverse women—Native American, Korean, Muslim, African-American and Latino—to congress.

It's another reminder that we must force ourselves to listen to young people. Theodore "Teddy" N. Landis (20), student chair of the Harvard Public Opinion Project, emphasized this point while stressing that increased young voter turnout in 2018 set a new bar for future elections. "I do think this sets a precedent that our politicians will need to listen to young people in the future," Landis said. "We're a demographic group with distinct policy preferences, and they'd be wise to pay attention to that."

***

As valiant and important as protest marches and voting are, I don't predict an immediate change in adult attitudes toward guns, mass shootings or the police killings of unarmed people of color. The forces of ignorance, fear, racism and the huge influx of money, bipartisanism and political manipulation won't be changed by marching or voting alone.

Peter Beinart—Newmark School of journalism professor, political commentator and contributor to the Atlantic, CNN and other media outlets—wrote: "The harsh truth is this: Racism often works. Cross-racial coalitions for economic justice are the exception in American history. Mobilizing white people to protect their racial dominance is the norm."

There is a powerful historical precedent of people—especially young people—standing up, voting, speaking out and publicly challenging wrong-headed adults or majority-thinking. Those who engaged in civil disobedience during the battles for worker's and women's rights, racial equality and justice, the unjust wars in Vietnam and Iraq and the "Occupy Wall Street" demonstrations were all on the right side of history.

"There is a powerful historical precedent of people—especially young people—standing up, voting, speaking out and publicly challenging wrong-headed adults or majority-thinking."

In Dec of 2018, thousands of Australian students from more than 200 schools skipped class to make their voices heard on the pressing issue of climate change. The idea for the country-wide "Strike 4 Climate Action" demonstration was the brainchild of two 14-year-old Melbourne students. Think of it. Two kids started a nation-wide march with thousands of their peers that will no doubt become a highlight in the history books.

We may not be able to instantly change a nation that's stubbornly clinging to ancient and broken systems, but what we *can* do is listen and react to the words and woes of young people. What we *must* do is ferret out what moves them, motivates them and worries them and support what they think they can change. We can do more than simply applaud their efforts. We can invest in their attitudes and attributes and inspire them to use their passions to create alternative systems.

We must affirm the pleas of our youth no matter their race, gender or economic standing. But, it's not only important to acknowledge their right to protest. We must also work to understand *why and how* they're protesting. If we dig deeper, we will hear more than young voices of anger, frustration or rebellion. We will better understand and help duplicate patterns of courage, creativity, resiliency, artistry, media savviness, strategic planning and purposeful unity.

***

Although some find it hard to listen when young people are loudly protesting our nation's hypocrisies and inconsistencies, it's crucial that we adults put our politics aside for a moment. We must work harder to see non-political acts of determination, strategy and creativity. If so, we might find better paths to stimulating a generation of young, engaged and empowered change-agents.

In Feb. 2018, Slate.com published an article that explored how education at Marjory Stoneman Douglas High School helped prepare its students for public conversations on gun control. The article, "They Were Trained for This Moment," written by Dahlia Lithwick, spoke to the burgeoning activist's eloquence and articulation and credited those attributes to extracurricular education taught at their school.

"Part of the reason the Stoneman Douglas students have become stars in recent weeks," Lithwick wrote, "is in no small part due to the fact that they are in a school system that boasts of a 'system-wide debate program that teaches extemporaneous speaking from an early age. Every middle and high school in the district has a forensics and public-speaking program. Coincidentally, some of the students had been preparing for debates on the issue of gun control this year, which explains, in part, why they could speak to the issues from day one."

Our collective goals should center around exploring and implementing innovative ways, like that of the Stoneman Douglas High, to inspire our nation's youth to use their inherent skills and voices to challenge and change their worlds.

Consider Roses in Concrete Community School in Oakland California. Established in 2014, the school was designed "for people of color by people of color" to improve the educational outcomes of black and Hispanic children. Founder Jeff Duncan-Andrade says the school was developed to compete with the fanciest independent schools by immersing students in art, extra-curricular activities and athletics with less emphasis on test prep.

"Culture is the defining difference," Duncan-Andrade said. "It's about acknowledging they'll love *The Cat in the Hat,* but also acknowledging they are black and brown kids in Oakland. So you'll see we hang the words of Malcolm X next to those of Dr. Seuss. To not talk about Black Lives Matter, even down to Kindergarten, [would be] a political decision. Our kids already know this stuff. They have had brothers, uncles shot." Duncan-Andrade added, "Students get everything they'd get from an elite private school, but from people who look like them."

Extracurricular activities at the performing arts community school delve deeply into the arts—modern jazz, dance, ballet, singing, learning to play musical instruments and arranging music. African, Latino and Native American traditions are incorporated in the school's curriculum.

While the mainstream media stubbornly and purposefully focused on vandalism and near riots during the St. Louis protests, it ignored valuable indications of what our young people offer society. A year after the death of Michael Brown, St. Louis Public Radio looked back to examine how young protestors combined arts and activism to articulate their confusion and pain.

The series looked at how artists in the region (and nationwide) were "examining and commemorating confusion and pain" through activism and art. Reporters Willis Ryder Arnold and Nancy Fowler noted how symbols, media images and slogans like the Gateway Arch and "hands up, don't shoot" were repurposed to show division, frustration, hope and unity. The visual and audio media images graphically and creatively illustrated Ferguson's exposed problems and perceived injustice within the criminal justice system.

Stoneman Douglas High School prepared its middle-to-upper-income students to challenge and change their worlds. The protests that followed Mike Brown's untimely death gave a disadvantaged young populace an organic platform that validated their right to creatively challenge injustice. The 2014 uprising not only served as a national and international template for bold, imaginative resistance; it led to the rise of a new generation of prominent young activists. Shaun King, DeRay Mckesso, Johnetta "Netta" Elzie, Brittany Packnett, Patrisse Cullors and Opal Tometi are among the names of BLM members or young demonstrators who became prominent after Mike Brown's death.

State Rep. Bruce Franks / Photo by Richard Reilly

Arguably, there is no other post-2014 story as inspirational as that of the tattooed Missouri politician Bruce Franks. No stranger to the game of hustle, Franks, 34, toiled as a cook, server, bartender, insurance agent, tax preparer and an up-and-coming rapper who went by the stage name "Ooops."

Franks, who had no interest in politics at the time, said he still doesn't know what compelled him to take to the streets on August

9, 2014, after hearing a 19-year-old had been shot by a Ferguson policeman. It was his son King's birthday. While looking at his smartphone, he said in a 2016 STL Magazine article, Franks saw Mike Brown's bloody body which remained on the street for some 4 hours.

"I told my wife, I need to be out there," Franks recalled in the interview.

He was "out there" for months, becoming a bold, photogenic fixture at the protests. He chronicled events in rap, including additional police shootings of black men after Brown's death. In December of 2014, Franks said St. Louis County and Berkeley police kicked him in the face and beat him with batons all while he was handcuffed face-down on the ground. It wasn't the only bloody confrontation Franks would have with police while demonstrating or trying to protect others under assault. Franks soon became a street legend. His raw street-rapping skills and activism were his launching-pad to politics.

The young outsider pulled off a political upset in 2016. He won a landslide victory in a rerun of a primary race against an entrenched politician, State Representative Penny Hubbard. A federal judge ordered a recount after allegations of serious irregularities with the absentee ballots clinched Hubbard's initial victory.

Today, Franks serves in the Missouri House of Representatives representing the 78th District. He's still a boisterous mainstay at protest rallies and, as it turns out, an effective politician with a knack for finding common ground with police and with politicians who do not share his "liberal" viewpoint, skin color or urban background.

With a devastating history of death and the loss of loved ones through senseless violence, Franks initially used rap lyrics to articulate and sooth his pain. His natural-born skills, validated through protesting, propelled him into a future with unlimited possibilities.

Bruce Franks is not an anomaly. His story should serve as a reminder that there are millions more like him. Many are maligned and many are ignored, but most are looking for someone or something that affirms that their feelings and opinions are valid and worthwhile.

***

What if we cease waiting for the system to correct itself? What if we institutionalize processes that can inspire and activate young people like those from *Marjory Stoneman Douglas High School,* Roses in Concrete Community School or all those fiery, artistic young voices and voters awakened by protesting like Bruce Franks?

The young people who are starting to vote, who are confronting overzealous police or injustice, reciting poetry, creating revolutionary rap lyrics, painting murals or defiantly gathering in our nation's streets reflect the passions, woes, frustrations and hopes of our youth. Truly listening, validating and proactively reacting to their pleas is a valuable step toward empowering an engaged citizenry while ensuring the sanctity of our democracy.

CHAPTER SEVEN
When They Are Accountable

Students, Michael Watson, Dashia Martin,
Myke King, Barry Goins
Photo by Benjamin Gandhi-Shepard

"Mr. Brown, what are you doing here?"

I don't know if Briana, one of my students, was really all that surprised to see me on Metro Bus #74. We both lived in the O'Fallon Park Neighborhood of North St. Louis. On many a day, I drove her or her classmates to or from class. All 25 youth enrolled that year (2013) knew "Mr. Brown" drove an unpredictable "hoopty." They also knew I lived in a neighborhood like theirs and faced the same money challenges as many of their parents. I'm very honest with the students about our struggles to raise funds for the program and pay their salaries.

"If the money's not there," I tell them, "we have to get creative to make it work!"

In other words, the kids know I'm an ordinary guy who's trying to empower them to do something extraordinary in their lives. They've seen me struggle to keep the program afloat. But they also understand it's a team effort. For me, it's important that they are just as accountable as I am for the program's success, not only for them but for generations to come.

Personally, I think it's important they know that someone who looks like them, lives where they live and grapples with the obstacles they face, can still make a difference. "Life..." as poet Langston Hughes phrased it, "ain't no crystal stair," especially in the rough and tumble world of entrepreneurism.

So, you might ask, "what could a guy with money troubles, who drove a crappy car and rode the bus on occasion possibly teach kids about success?"

My answer is three-fold. First, I've lived long enough to know that current situations do not define us. I've been to the top of my professional career. I've had the limelight and stature but still felt a huge void. My "success," if you will, is directly attributed to my ability to adapt, to be creative and employ my inherent skills. So, yeah, I may live a challenging life, but it's much richer because I have this rare and wonderful opportunity to impact the lives of young people.

To be clear, I'm not the only positive influence in their lives. Through the Sweet Potato Project, we've brought all sorts of successful entrepreneurs and professionals to class to share their stories, advice and expertise. Lastly, I maintain that part of being an entrepreneur is having the grit to overcome and outlast hardships and creatively use whatever talent, skill or gifts we have to beat back difficulties and make our own way.

The students seem to appreciate the fact that I think they can make great change. Maybe it's because most educators and adults in their lives don't talk to them like I do. Rarely do we hold young people responsible and accountable for the positive change they need in their lives and communities. Oftentimes, adults, without listening, decide what's best for young people.

St. Louis has been at the top of the "Most Dangerous Cities" list for decades. As I wrote this chapter, the number of homicides in our city had topped 200. I believe that we will never effectively reduce crime or murder in low-income neighborhoods until the people living in them can create alternative ways to educate, inspire and economically empower young people. I maintain that we have a yeoman's task before us. Collectively, we must adopt a new mindset of economic independence. Extraordinary, ordinary people—not the government—must take the lead in creating environments where young people are surrounded by positive adults and productive self-sustaining activity. We must foster a new attitude of ownership and investment in neighborhoods where our kids grow up. Most important, we must allow our youth to draft their own futures.

"We will never effectively reduce crime or murder in low-income neighborhoods until the people living in them can create alternative ways to educate, inspire and economically empower young people."

Let me give you a couple of examples of how we reinforce this theme at SPP:

In one exercise, I asked students to imagine themselves owning several vacant city lots. "See yourself building a home and growing food on your property," I said. "There are a lot of young people in our neighborhoods who hang out drinking or smoking dope on vacant properties," I remind them before asking if they'd accept this behavior as property owners.

"Hell, naw," one student, Antonio responded. "This is my property. Ain't nobody gonna mess with what's mine, believe that!"

The implied threat aside, Antonio's desire to protect what he deemed valuable is worth acknowledgment and further exploration. Other students offered more diplomatic remedies: talking to vagrants, posting signs or simply showing other young people how to acquire land and grow food. That way, one student explained, there'd be a group dynamic where they would enforce their own rules instead of depending on police or punitive political legislation.

The student's openness to neighborhood accountability speaks to the larger vision of our program. There are thousands of vacant lots in the St. Louis region. One of our North St. Louis Alderman, John C. Muhammad, introduced legislation to sell vacant city lots and abandoned homes to disadvantaged residents and developers for $1. As of this writing, the proposed legislation had received huge push-back from fellow politicians. Another bill pushed by Muhammad would have enacted a zoning change where government dollars would have gone toward creating "agricultural zones" in low-income neighborhoods. That bill went nowhere.

For me, the lack of momentum on these ideas represents the need for a new, holistic, empowering vision that places the onus of accountability in the hands of the demographic most in need of social and economic salvation. In St. Louis, politicians stubbornly cling to the idea that only wealthy developers or major "big box" developments can transform neighborhoods. Therefore, city leaders push tax incentives to help corporations and wealthy developers enhance or revitalize neighborhoods that only they deem "sustainable." This is but one reason why the poorest neighborhoods in North St. Louis have seen no major developments in more than 60 years.

The lack of industry in metropolitan neighborhoods throughout the country has had a disproportionate, negative impact on inner-cities. However, because everyone eats; growing, packaging and distributing fresh food can be a viable economic engine for hard-hit communities. It is a way to organically create jobs and increase small businesses, but the focus must be on ground-up, grassroots participation. Training young people to be pioneers in this movement is essential for future development.

I read of a couple programs across the country where new homes were built on vacant land for under $40,000. The Tiny Homes initiative in Detroit, for example, has a program where people can own homes outright after seven years. Similar initiatives are spreading across the country, including St. Louis. But, to date, the emphasis has been on Tiny Homes for the homeless or veterans. This is well and good, but what if the Tiny Homes idea was extended to instigate home and landownership for millennials?

Imagine bold, nurturing environments where youngsters as young as 21 were given tax incentives and subsidies to own vacant land and new, affordable homes, where they can become food-growers and producers. What may happen if urban youth were shown how to start new businesses and create jobs in their own neighborhoods? Imagine the level of pride and ownership if a line of food was packaged and manufactured from North St. Louis. I predict a sea-change in neighborhoods simply based on the idea of investing in poor and young people and holding them accountable for the safety, revitalization and economic vitality of disadvantaged neighborhoods.

***

When They Make the Rules

I tried something new in the first years of SPP's operations. I asked the students to develop their own set of rules and punishments if anyone acted out. The new policy was put to the test when two students, male and female, got into an argument which resulted in the boy calling the girl the B-word. That incident and a few others didn't exactly produce the results I desired.

"It was a good thing that we set the rules and boundaries, but it really wasn't that effective," my student Charles said. "I'm not really fond of that word. I don't think a male should treat a female like that. If your Dad called your mom the B-word, it would be like he's disrespecting her. For him to call her out-of-her-name, that wasn't right. Also, we're a team. We're doing this together and there's no need for teammates to be fighting each other."

"I feel like it was useless," Marquitta added. "Nobody followed the rules. Things were still being done that shouldn't have been done and words were used that shouldn't have been used. The rules were pointless. We came up with rules that we didn't even follow ourselves."

Keon agreed but added additional thoughts: "Nobody really followed the rules, but it can be enforced a bit more and we can make different rules with slight loopholes that don't give just a one-sided conversation. If I violated a rule, I'd like to be able to tell my side and say why I did this

120

or that, so I just won't be considered a bad person."

Barry didn't think the idea was good either but he recognized the merits of our approach: "The idea was good. It gave us a sense of empowerment and sent a signal from the adults that we're giving you our trust and letting you all run something. But it didn't follow through the way we planned because the kids didn't follow the rules."

Elesha, the young woman who was insulted, said she learned something from the whole situation: "I feel like the situation was addressed in a decent manner, but I disagreed with the way it was handled for personal reasons. But I learned to forgive and forget from my peers while continuing the program. They taught me a valuable lesson about just letting things go."

The self-rule process didn't work because the students were much less forgiving and tolerant than I was. They didn't give a hoot about the factors that may influence negative behavior. "If you act out, you're fired," was the gist of their recommendations. But, as Marquitta noted, some of the kids who were breaking the rules created the rules. I had to remind them that many of them would have been out of the program if I had adhered to their sanctions.

The experiment led me to explore the possibilities of self-rule. An essay by Paul Meunier, the director of services for the Youth Intervention Programs Association at the time, proved helpful. Although Meunier wrote about holding youth in the juvenile justice system accountable for the offenses they may commit, his analysis about adolescents spoke to me.

"We are ignoring a basic biological fact that the brain is not fully developed until about 24 years of age," Meunier wrote, adding, "Without a fully developed cortex, youth are more impulsive, lack the ability to tie actions to long-term consequences, and are hypersensitive to the opinions of others."

I agree with Meunier's admonition that, as a society, we need to give much thought to how we hold young people, not just young offenders, accountable. Whereas I left it up to the students to make their own rules, Meunier emphasized that it's critical to have peer groups and caring adults involved who can influence and help youth navigate the process.

"Good caregivers show youth that they sincerely care about them. This includes providing tough love and teaching empathy. At the same time, youth need peer groups and friends who have a sense of hope and optimism for the future."

We will continue to work in this area. I will try to get students to practice empathy and not just act as strict disciplinarians. Many times, I've had to explain the background of an unruly student to the students or stress our desire to help reverse bad behaviors. I preach accountability and responsibility and encourage older students to become leaders and role models.

"Good caregivers show youth that they sincerely care about them. This includes providing tough love and teaching empathy. At the same time, youth need peer groups and friends who have a sense of hope and optimism for the future."—Paul Meunier, Youth Intervention Programs Association

For example, during the 2017 summer session, a new student stole a pair of earphones from another teen in the program. The perpetrator was bi-polar, had been raised in foster homes and could barely read. I learned all this after sitting with the boy's case-worker. He apologized for the crime but that wasn't good enough. I told him that he had to fess up and apologize to the victim and the entire class and let them decide his fate. To his credit, he did. The other students graciously accepted his apology but also told him he'd hurt the reputation of "their" program. To my delight, a couple of the senior students started looking out for the boy, helping him with assignments and making sure he stayed engaged and felt like he was a crucial part of the team.

This outcome of that incident spoke to Meunier's advice about tough love and teaching empathy. It feeds my belief that there is a way, with the help of caring adults, to show young people that they can indeed make the rules and provide a template for community ownership.

***

Tapping into Their Inherent Talents

It seems that millennials have a natural entrepreneurial spirit. According to a University of Phoenix survey, 63 percent of people in their 20s either own or want to own their own businesses with 55 percent hoping to be entrepreneurs of the future. The study underscored the fact that people under 30 "have more of an entrepreneurial itch than their older counterparts."

Many poor, immigrant, black and Latino communities have always participated in the underground economy, also known as "shadow" markets or the "black economy." It's a system where goods or services are exchanged but not reported to the IRS. Though rooted in notorious dealings such as bootlegging and prostitution, modern examples include babysitting, selling baked goods, doing hair or lawn care, car repair, food service, housekeeping or construction and, yes, selling narcotics. Though some activities are necessary in disadvantaged neighborhoods, the underground economy results in huge losses of revenues to the government.

I have worked with young people who demonstrate natural desires and skills to make money, with many doing so "off the books." My personal goal is to take the mystique out of doing business correctly and help them transform their hustles into legitimate business enterprises.

The Sweet Potato Project was designed to tap into those creative survival skills that come with being born and raised poor. Most of our students have no idea how they already influence modern culture. Their music, slang and clothing styles have been co-opted and enjoyed by mainstream society. You can't go to a sporting event without hearing hip-hop or popular R&B music. Our kids, no matter how poor, manage to find the deals to stay sharp with the latest styles of tennis shoes, shirts, skirts, hair-dos and much more.

In class, I ask students to develop their own media campaigns. Within two hours, they come up with products or ideas that could possibly make millions. During a 2013 session, we had a chemist visit the class during one of these exercises. One of the teams came up with an eye and hair color-changing candy product. The chemist sat in class with his mouth agape. One of his colleagues, he told us, was working on getting a patent for a similar eye-color-changing pill. This, my friends, is the sort of genius that's walking our streets, filling our prisons or being mostly ignored or unnoticed in society.

To foster a generation of responsible youth, we adults most first hold ourselves accountable. Young people didn't create the systems that routinely rob them of their innocence and opportunities. As legalized segregation was defeated, parents and grandparents of today's black youth evacuated long-populated black neighborhoods to seek better living and educational conditions. There was a time when blacks had no choice but to build and support their own businesses. Today, many poor black neighborhoods are devoid of black-owned businesses and, most importantly, daily examples of hard-working entrepreneurs who look like them.

Everyone—the concerned and connected—can play a role in reversing the negative trends that disproportionately impact at-risk youth. However, I maintain that African Americans must take the lead in establishing alternative systems designed for the best outcomes for our children.

The Sweet Potato Project is but one viable approach. Again, everybody eats. So let's educate a generation of youth to grow, package, process and distribute fresh food and food products. I will revisit and expand on this topic more toward the end of this book. But, for now, let's just say a money-making, food-based undertaking is a sound, common sense way to empower future generations to reenergize long-ignored and underdeveloped areas of any city. Most importantly, it's a vision that can help our youth realize and capitalize off the notion that they are responsible and accountable for their own success.

REFLECTION

John Collins-Muhammad and Restoring "Higher Purpose"

January 2018

Photo Courtesy of John Collins Muhammad

"Are you the exception or the rule?"

John Collins-Muhammad chuckled softly before answering my question. At 26-years-old, articulate and ambitious, no doubt he'd been asked that question before. Young black men who seem to have it together are often asked why they are "different." Mostly, the question comes from curious whites who believe they've contradicted the stereotype.

I got the impression Collins-Muhammad knew where I was headed with the query. I told him I wanted to interview him for this book because he was young and accomplished. We met in an office of St. Peters AME Church where he, the pastor and several community members operate an emergency shelter providing cots, hot meals and clothing for the homeless.

In 2017, Collins-Muhammad was elected alderman of the 21st Ward in North St. Louis. At the time, he was the youngest elected official in the history of the state of Missouri. I was immediately impressed with the young aldermen who, in his first year in office, introduced two aldermanic bills aimed at putting vacant city property in the hands of low-income people for $1 and another that would establish agricultural zones so urban farmers could receive federal, state and city funds to grow fresh food and beautify disadvantaged neighborhoods.

"I am them and they are me," he answered confidently.

According to the alderman, poor black youth have the same potential as he does. The defining factor of a productive life, he added, is "education, guidance and mentorship."

"It's having someone to walk you through and coach you through life experiences when you're young. Someone to almost hold your hand and say 'no, don't do it this way, I tried that, you can do it differently,'" Collins-Muhammad said. "That creates the channel. That takes us back to what the community used to be. When you have someone who cares about you, cares about your community who will invest in you, a young person can move differently."

Collins-Muhammad was born in the Greater Ville neighborhood of North St. Louis. The historic area was once home to thousands of African Americans who could not reside in segregated parts of the city. Long before his birth, "the Ville" was a place of prominence and pride, a place where blacks found employment in their own neighborhood through institutions like Annie Malone's Poro Beauty College, Homer G. Phillips Hospital and Sumner High School.

Listening to his life story reminded me that anyone in any situation can inspire a kid. Collins-Muhammad's father was incarcerated throughout his entire young life, yet he still managed to be the major motivator and mentor for his son. Muhammad said his aunts, Linda and LaTonia Collins, "adopted" him and regularly took him to visit his father in prison. With convictions of murder, drug trafficking, kidnapping, arson and parole violation, his dad was destined for a life behind bars. The father, however, concealed that fact from his only son.

"He'd lie to me. He would always say he was coming home," Collins-Muhammad reminisced. "He would say he was working on something to get out early. Looking back, I think he told me those things to give me faith and hope."

His father died in prison in 2007. Before his death, though, Muhammad said his father "schooled" him, dropping pearls of wisdom that he later learned originated from the Holy Koran. His father was an even bigger influence after he had a heart attack and passed away.

"All his belongings were shipped to our home. I started going through his things and I found a Koran," Collins-Muhammad recalled. "I had no clue what it was, I could barely understand its contents. But I wanted to understand. Since my father had this book, I figured he was a Muslim, so I reflected on different things he said, the letters he wrote or our conversations on the phone. I started to see a connection between Islam and what he shared with me."

The alderman described his younger self as "a curious kid."

"I loved reading and watching documentaries on anything, from dolphins to the Civil War, anything dealing with history, science, social or economic factors...I was just fascinated with it all."

Although his father was influential in his life, the reality was that Collins-Muhammad was raised in an all-female household. He didn't really know how a man should act or behave, he told me. So he sought those experiences outside the home. He joined a gang, but that experience ended quickly—within weeks in fact. Fear of his mother finding out and the fact that gangs gave him no positive reinforcement led him to seek male tutelage elsewhere.

He was raised in the Baptist Church where his mother enrolled him in various mentorship programs. But, Collins-Muhammad added, they seemed "watered down, disingenuous" and didn't speak to him. Convinced that his father was a Muslim, his son sought a similar path. He recognized a sense of pride and belonging through notable figures such as Malcolm X, Minister Louis Farrakhan, Muhammad Ali and Stockley Carmichael (later Kwame Ture).

At the age of 15, Collins-Muhammad joined the Moorish Science Temple. There, he learned what he considered Islamic-based philosophies. But the organization, he added, didn't feel "legitimately Muslim." Therefore, he joined the Nation of Islam (NOI) Mosque #28 on West Florissant Avenue in North St. Louis and converted to Islam in 2016.

The religion provided the foundation and roadmap Collins-Muhammad needed to move confidently forward. After graduating high school, he enrolled at Lincoln University where he studied political science and international affairs. Two former Missouri state representatives, T.D. El-Amin and Rodney Hubbard Jr., both Muslims, took the unknown but burgeoning political student under their wings. Hubbard, a Lincoln University alumnus, communicated with Collins-Muhammad's professors and paid for the student's campaign for class president in 2009. He lost, but never forgot the senior politician's investment in his endeavors.

Collins-Muhammad recalled another occasion in 2008, when he accompanied El-Amin at a local grocery store. The state rep greeted a constituent who had recently lost her son to violence and was frantically trying to raise money to bury the child.

"Without a moment's hesitation, TD offered to pay for the whole thing," Collins-Muhammad reminisced. "And I've seen him do things like that—these acts of generosity—a thousand times, but that was the first and I was in awe."

El-Amin and Hubbard's attention, mentorship and political activities helped steer Collins-Muhammad in the direction of public service.

While in college, his family moved to the 21st ward, which includes parts of College Hill, Kingsway East, North Riverfront, O'Fallon and Penrose—all predominantly black-populated but mostly disadvantaged neighborhoods of North St. Louis.

Collins-Muhammad graduated and got married in 2015. Before marriage, however, he went into the arena of public protest after Michael Brown's death. Simultaneously, he shifted into public policy, doing campaign work for politicians and labor organizations like the AFL-CIO. Influenced by El-Amin and Hubbard, he threw his hat in the ring for Missouri State Representative of the 77th District in 2016. "Enough is enough," a quote borrowed from Malcolm X, was the mantra of his campaign. As part of a trend of young people across the nation rising to seek political offices, Collins-Muhammad set out to show that young people could indeed make positive, long-lasting change in politics.

"I wholeheartedly believe there is a new trend going on, which is awesome," Collins-Muhammad said in a 2016 Daily Kos article. "I know people who still subscribe to the old tenants of politics might feel otherwise. They have hesitation, citing that young people don't have enough experience or knowledge of 'the system,' but that's the exact type of ancient thinking that will hinder progress."

"Government should work for the people, not against them," Collins-Muhammad said, adding, "The times are too serious, the stakes are too high. Our work will not be met easily and the challenges and issues we face are going to require tough choices. We need to cast off the worn-out ideas and politics of the past, put an end to petty grievances, and begin the work of rebuilding our communities."

Alas, Collins-Muhammad suffered a crushing defeat. He lost the state rep race by less than 800 votes. A year later, 21st Ward alderman Antonio French decided to run for mayor, which meant he had to vacate his seat. Voters inside and outside the ward who remembered Collins-Muhammad's run for state rep implored the then 25-year-old to seek the aldermanic seat. Still brooding from his loss, Collins-Muhammad was hesitant to enter the race. A conversation with former alderman and long-time public policy advisor Mike Jones helped change his mind.

"He (Jones) told me that being the alderman of the 21st ward was like being a senator from New York," Collins-Muhammad recalled. "Everything is here, Jones said. Highway 70, Natural Bridge, Grand Blvd. It's the perfect location for economic development. He said that all I needed to do to be successful was maintain relationships with the people. I think he was telling me the ward needed someone they know, trust and someone who will be there when they call."

With a war chest of less than $1,500 and assistance from Mobilize Missouri, a group of activists who took part in Bernie Sanders' presidential campaign, Collins-Muhammad won the race by a mere 29 votes. Vowing to bring "new blood, a new perspective, and a new way to look at things," the freshman alderman has worked steadily and quickly to live up to his creed. Asked to describe his political approach, Collins-Muhammad relies on one word: "Hope. We're hoping to rebuild the ward block-by-block, street-by-street. We're hoping to come up with real solutions, a plan to tackle crime. We're hoping to have more block units and neighborhood organizations working in unison with one another; hoping that everyone plays a part in making the 21st Ward a better place for all."

Collins-Muhammad talks the refreshing, bold verbiage of the young and optimistic. He imagines neighborhoods in his ward becoming the "Black Meccas" of the city, "Missouri's Harlem," he said wistfully. This was the story, the vision, the passion and sheer resolve that prompted my "acceptation or the rule" question. Never mind the skepticism, doubt or challenges based on age or experience. I wanted to know the collective ingredients needed to inspire a cadre of young John Collins-Muhammad's in troubled black neighborhoods. Moving beyond the stereotypes and personally taking young people by the hand, he says, is a great starting point.

"Young black people are only stereotypes because no one is investing in them. There's untapped potential in people like me," Collins-Muhammad stressed. "But if no one tells them 'hey, your life matters, you matter, what you do matters,' we're not going to care about the next person. If my life doesn't matter, then no one's life matters."

Listening to the young aldermen reinforced for me the mountainous task ahead if we are to truly spur a generation of young people with similar visions and aspirations. We must go back to go forward. We must build self-sufficient communities of the past where, because of segregation and racism, black people had no choice but do-for-self and dictate their own destinies. Collins-Muhammad spoke to this in the Daily Koz piece: "What's missing in so many black neighborhoods today is a common purpose," he said. "We need to restore a sense of higher purpose.

CHAPTER EIGHT

When They Know Money

"Damn right I like the life I live because I went from negative to positive."—Biggie Smalls/Notorious BIG

Photo Courtesy of the Sweet Potato Project

Rapper, songwriter, record producer and multi-million-dollar businessman Jay-Z (born Shawn Corey Carter) isn't exactly a youngster. But, for someone who's been in the entertainment business since his early 20s and has legends of young fans, Jay-Z's words merit attention.

With his 2017 album "4:44," Jay-Z parlays his experience as a former drug dealer and all-time savvy hustler into a template for urban success. He preaches in one song, "Legacy," that building generational wealth is the key for economic salvation. In another cut, "The Story of O.J.," the rapper warns that no one, including black celebrities like the fallen football great or himself, can escape the reality of race relations in America.

The ballad speaks to the backwards "get rich or die trying" mentality that many young, naïve people passionately embrace. It's a message they may already hear from adults but when Jay-Z, a former drug dealer, sings it, it has more authenticity. Laced within the album's lyrics are lessons in strategic investing, financial-planning and owning real estate and fine art rather than depreciating items like fancy cars or shiny jewelry. While grappling with his own shortcomings as a husband and father on the "Family Feud" track, Jay-Z raps that "a man that don't take care his family can't be rich."

The entrepreneur who, according to Forbes, is worth more than $800 million, uses his experience to encourage blacks to lift each other up financially by supporting black-owned businesses and buying property in their own neighborhoods. Early in "The Story of O.J.," for example, Jay-Z reveals a lost opportunity to buy available property in Brooklyn before the neighborhood rebounded: "I could have bought a place in Dumbo before it was Dumbo for like 2 million. That same building today is worth 25 million. Guess how I'm feeling? Dumbo."

***

Hip-Hop artists and rappers receive a lot of flak for promoting materialistic, misogynistic and violent lifestyles. As warranted as some of this criticism is, I think we do a disservice when we generalize and demonize the entire rap community. Personally, I don't have high expectations of youngsters who happen to break into the multi-billion-dollar, sensationalized rap game. I mean, they're kids. When I was in my late teens and early 20s, sex, money and survival were themes that preoccupied a lot of my mental space. I expect kids raised around or influenced by violence to rap and even romanticize the vicious worlds they navigate. I assume they'll amplify and glorify lifestyles that are irresponsible, risqué and salacious. Those raised in a violent society probably won't rift about flowers, rainbows, healthy marriages or creating a better world for all mankind.

Still, I think adults should make a conscious effort to try and give young people the benefit of reason. You may detest hip-hop music, but maybe, just maybe, young people are receiving messages that resonate with their frustrations or aspirations. Some hip-hop artists like J-Z, Biggie Smalls and others have used their platforms to occasionally promote and encourage their young fans to reclaim their lives and communities. Mixed with the sexist, violent and reckless rhetoric are real life insights and pearls of wisdom about responsibly building personal and community wealth even if born impoverished.

"Adults should make a conscious effort to try and give young people the benefit of reason. You may detest hip-hop music, but maybe, just maybe, young people are receiving messages that resonate with their frustrations or aspirations."

If we are serious about nurturing a generation of youth who will reclaim and remake communities of chaos, perhaps we should look for innovative ways to tune in, listen and utilize the musical messages they receive from popular rap and hip-hop artists.

In a "Millennial Money" blog post, founder and author of *Financial Freedom,* Grant Sabatier, confessed that a lot of what he learned about personal finance came from rappers. Reading the post helped me imagine ways to have conversations with young people based on the words of their favorite artists. I've condensed and revised some of Sabatier's words, but here are a few examples he provided:

Biggie Smalls on the freedom money allows: *Take a better stand. Put money in my mom's hand. Get my daughter this college plan, so she don't need no man.*

Kanye West on fiscal irresponsibility: *I want to act ballerific like it's all terrific | I got a couple past-due bills, I won't get specific | I got a problem with spendin' before I get it.*

Jay-Z on creative side hustles: *I sell ice in the winter, I sell fire in hell, I am a hustler baby, I'll sell water to a well.*

Drake on wealth diversification: *Oh well, guess you win some and lose some, as long as the outcome is income.*

The point I'm attempting to make here is that we must use all the examples, reminders and resources possible to adopt new lexicons of relevant conversations aimed at helping urban youth use money for their personal and collective empowerment.

***

Cheryl Walker
Community Development Director
Stifel Bank & Trust

During the summer of 2017, I took my students to a financial literacy class conducted by Cheryl Walker, Community Development director for Stifel Bank & Trust. As we entered the Excel Center in the Old North neighborhood, we were greeted with a generous buffet of deli meat, croissants, fruit, drinks and snacks. The students sat facing a huge TV screen already tuned to the YouTube channel. Walker asked the students what they wanted to hear. They shouted out a litany of artists like Drake, Kendrick Lamar and Beyoncé. Walker patiently responded to their requests while engaging them in conversations about the artist's music, lives and latest adventures.

After about a half hour of casual music-based conversations, Walker effortlessly switched modes. For the next hour or so, I watched as she and my students discussed the importance of financial knowledge: saving money at early ages, dealing with negative credit scores, reducing debt and improving credit with the same ease and lilt of the previous hip-hop conversations.

Walker segued from the fantasy lifestyles of the rich and famous to the real world of paying rent, cable, car note and student loan bills while still managing to save enough to live worry-free. The students were immediately engaged and involved. I listened as they talked openly about financial challenges and opportunities from their own vantage points.

It was a marvel to behold.

After the session, I quizzed Walker on the method she uses to engage young people. "It's all about trust. I speak their language," she responded. "We can cut to the chase because I know what they don't know. I know what they need to know, and I know how to say it." Walker added. "Why in the world would I bring them a flow chart when I can just say, 'look, you make a hundred dollars a week, put $10 of that in the bank.' Then I show them what that 10 percent looks like in their world and lives."

Walker, who conducts financial literacy and "Money Smart" classes for young, low-income and middle-class people throughout the region, is the real deal. Her authenticity is based on her own experiences and revelations she's found in the world of financial empowerment.

She learned the power of equity after selling a home she bought for $50,000 in 1986 for $92,000 in 2001. Walker and her husband started buying properties two years later. She took out a loan on her car to rehab one her rental properties. "We bought it for $7,000. We fixed that one up and bought another and another. Those houses started making money to pay off the loans we had generated. Eventually, by 2005, we had 11 houses and it was easy to do. If your credit is good, if you're in the 700 Club (credit score) you qualify for even lower interest rates. Our goal was to get out of debt and those houses were assets used to reduce our debt."

The equity revelation set Walker on an unplanned course of enlightenment.

"I couldn't believe it," Walker recalled, referring to her equity windfall. "So, I said to the Lord, 'I'm going to teach others.' I started teaching others what equity is and what it can do to empower you."

Walker immersed herself in knowledge-sharing. She started consulting on the art of buying cheap properties, fixing them up and renting them out to cover the small acquisition loans. This was done without pay, however. She had the experience but lacked the credentials to qualify as a recognized financial consultant. That all changed in 2007 after she applied for a job at Edward Jones financial services firm. "The author of *Rich Dad, Poor Dad* (Robert Kiyosaki) said, 'if you want to learn something, go work for someone with that information.' So, I did. I was hired at Edward Jones as a retirement and education specialist. So now I had real estate and investment knowledge."

> "So, I said to the Lord, 'I'm going to teach others.' I started teaching others what equity is and what it can do to empower you."

Walker's quest for investment information continued. She accepted a position with an organization that helped low-income people secure loans and save their homes from foreclosure. That job exposed her to lending institutions looking for creative ways to finance people with challenged credit. She interviewed with other mortgage companies, but it was in 2012 at Stifel where an interviewee put a label on her unique talents. "She said 'there's a name for what you do, it's called community development.' I said, 'Oh, my God, really?' And they hired me on the spot."

The rest, as they say, is history. Walker developed relationships with churches, public schools and government and community organizations such as the city's Office of Financial Empowerment, the Urban League and Better Family Life. With a diverse portfolio of financial education, she's become St. Louis' go-to person to help anyone, especially low-income individuals, buy homes, get loans, fix spotty credit and build solid financial nest eggs.

To that end, Walker has used creative and culturally-relevant events like her *Our Money Matters* musical and a community event based on the popular Monopoly board game to teach the values of buying property, saving and investing money. One of her greatest passions, however, is educating people at early ages. For Walker, this outreach is personal. "They (youth) are my future. For me, it's an investment. The media tends to focus on the most negative, dire things in our community. The majority, however, are children who want to know what I'm saying. They want to do better than their parents, they want to make a difference."

***

Walker touches on a profound revelation I discovered while working with at-risk youth: they want to do better. They really do want to help their siblings and peers. And they want to be successes in their own neighborhoods. Most just don't know how.

In his album *2014 Forest Hills Drive*, rapper J. Cole tells the oh so familiar "rags to riches" tale but cautiously adds a warning about chasing money without at the sake of happiness:

Always gon' be a bigger house somewhere, but...

Long as the people in [it] love you dearly

Always gon' be a [car] that's better than the one you got

Always gon' be some clothes that's fresher than the ones you rock

Always gon' be a [girl] that's [more attractive] out there on the tours

But you ain't never gon' be happy till you love yours…

Sometimes rap artists also acknowledge that they do indeed contribute to dehumanizing racial stereotypes. Consider Bronx-native and spoken word artist and rapper D-Black (born David Roberts). In his urban/Afrocentric piece titled "I apologize," D-Black addresses the contradictions and cultural sacrifices many young hip-hop artists believe they must make to grasp success in the warped entertainment world:

I apologize

I apologize for being a rapper that floods your airwaves with songs that deprave

Your kids, mine, making them mental slaves…

I apologize for promoting company's lack of respect for me

Stretching out their demographics, increasing their currency

I apologize for demeaning women when some of ya'll don't deserve it

Prostituting ya'll on wax as a means of making profit

I apologize for exploiting my hood when I should be explaining it

Using it as a stepping stone when I should be saving it

…I Sambo on tracks, manifesting buffoonery,

Cause these black companies can't offer what these white ones

are paying me Rhythmic masochists, gyrating to degradation,
souls missing something like single-parent housing, now you
know why today's black youth is unbalanced, say hello to our
future gang members, corner drug dealers, listening to me Mike
Jones and Jim Jones, tryna figure out who's the better father
figure...

D-Black's offering speaks to a problem of our own creation. Our youth are indeed "unbalanced," but who created the backwards conditions they must navigate? How can we expect positivity when many youth have been raised amongst continuous negativity? Remember, we are dealing with the products of generational poverty and mass incarceration. We see the remnants of communities that have been under siege since the end of slavery. We are experiencing the latest phase of a generational social experiment based on the premise of first turning human beings into chattel. And, secondly, affording the chattel's offspring with sub-human treatment, violence, oppression, segregation and all the baggage associated with second-class citizenship.

"I apologize for exploiting my hood when I should be explaining it. Using it as a stepping stone when I should be saving it..." —David Roberts (AKA D-Black)

Trust me, I'm not expecting adults to become hip-hop aficionados. Some of the music is simply ridiculous and unacceptable. I get it. Still, I'm asking that we try and understand the music our kids enjoy. While driving my students around during our summer program, I purposely tune my radio to popular R&B or hip-hop stations. As the students bop and sing in the vehicle, I ask them about the meaning of the words or lyrics we hear. This oftentimes leads to interesting discussions about their lives, neighborhoods, peers and societal conditions.

What if we adults took the extra effort to engage our young people through the music they adore? I derived much of the information for this chapter by simply Googling topics like "rappers & wealth" or "hip-hop and financial literacy." This can be a holistic start for many of us.

After years of research and writing about the conditions of African Americans, I am convinced that our only salvation is to reclaim, revitalize and recreate community-based systems. We need new systems that address or replace institutionalized deficiencies that keep black people trapped in unjust and underserving economic, criminal justice and educational paradigms. I dream of a world where "at-risk" youth are provided just as many opportunities to succeed as there are to fail. I will get more into this vision in the last chapter, "When they are Empowered."

For now, I'll just say that this mission must start with today's youth. As Walker said, they are our future. We must find ways, like her methods, to institutionalize new financial conversations and avenues for empowerment. We can do this by listening, learning, tuning in, expanding on the social, pop cultural and everyday messages to make them relevant to our kid's future and ours.

CHAPTER NINE

When They Are Empowered

"If the Negro is to be free, he must move down into the inner-resources of his own soul and sign with a pen and ink of self-assertive manhood his own Emancipation Proclamation!"

- Dr. Martin Luther King, Jr.

SPP student, Charnell Hurn
Photo by Benjamin Gandhi-Shepard

"Local Columnist Attacked by Angry Mob at MLK Event."

The imaginary headline flitted across my mind during a Jan. 14, 2006 Dr. Martin Luther King, Jr celebratory event. Panelists included celebrities such as ABC News correspondent Vicki Mabrey; Judge Mablean Ephriam, star of TV's "Divorce Court;" former County Prosecutor Bob McCulloch; author Omar Tyree and Missouri Congressman William Lacy Clay Jr.

Each explained what they thought blacks should do to keep "King's Dream" alive. To me, the forum seemed more like a gripe session than a "call to action" as it was billed. Comments ranged from dissing deadbeat dads, young rappers who make "booty-shaking" videos, drug dealers to out-of-control black youth. As moderator, I felt the need to add another perspective:

"I believe we, as a race, are exactly where we're supposed to be..."

Before finishing the thought, a communal gasp rose from the 300-or-so member audience. All the panelists snapped their heads in my direction. "What?" one loudly exclaimed. The room exploded with a melee of shouts, insults and finger-pointing. A local minister jumped to his feet. "No, no, Mr. Brown. You don't know what you're saying!" An elderly woman shouted from the back of the auditorium: "Drugs and gangs are killing our community!" Yet another angry voice accused me of "Defending crack dealers!"

It wasn't exactly my shining moment. Still, all these years later, I stand by my words. Of course, we can "do better" as a race. And, yes, many of our young people are involved in negative, self-destructive behaviors. However, if we look at the timeline of our collective progress, I still maintain that we are exactly where we're supposed to be.

After nearly 400 years of slavery, racial oppression, segregation and government-sanctioned racism, can we, as a people, really expect to be universally healed? After all, we've only had 50 years or so of "independence," and that's if we start with the civil rights legislation passed in the late 1960s. Generational poverty is still a debilitating mainstay. Since the 1970s, many middle-class blacks have abandoned their neighborhoods and closed black businesses to seek government-granted opportunities in suburbia or jobs with white-owned corporations.

As presidents have come and gone, African Americans are forever fighting for mere existence. By some estimates, more than 50 percent of our collective gains were lost amidst the Great Recession of 2007-2009 which was fueled by a collapsed housing market. With such damaging social and economic factors beating us down for decades, can we really feign surprise that uninspired, mis-directed youth have turned to negative ways to survive?

Yes, we are where we're supposed to be given the generational inequities we continue to navigate. Our children did not create the nefarious world they inhabit today. We adults left them environments where drug-dealing seems more applicable than legitimate business-building. We've turned them over to inadequate, institutionalized systems: educational, economic and criminal justice—many of which have been specifically designed for their demise.

I maintain that the social and economic landscape won't be better until we, as a collective, commit to fixing it. As Dr. King said in the opening quote above, if are to be truly free, we must move with "self-assertive" action to enact our own form of collective emancipation.

***

One word summarizes my call for mass change: empowerment. I believe we must adopt a comprehensive agenda that prepares, nurtures and empowers our youth to use their inherent skills to beat institutionalized odds and create their own opportunities in their own neighborhoods.

Deindustrialization has had a devasting impact on many major urban cities, including St. Louis. The aftereffect of labor-intensive manufacturing jobs sent overseas to companies with much lower wages and lower industry standards in the '70s, '80s and '90s coupled with technological inventions that require less manual labor has left many metropolitan areas, especially black areas, desolate and broken—with our kids devoid of real life examples of do-for-self success.

I was raised in poor areas of the city but there were also nice, stable middle-class black neighborhoods where adults worked for automotive, meat-packaging, the Post Office or other government agencies. I was raised at a time when segregation was breathing its last breath. Yet, it was still a time when blacks had no choice but do business with one another. There was a healthy sense of entrepreneurship in my day where vendors set up neighborhood shops or walked the block selling everything from ice cream to candy to coal to watermelons to fried cracklin'.

Integration and deindustrialization created major shifts in community dynamics. When I walked the block as a kid, I met black convenience store, funeral home and other business owners. Some gave kids like me a couple bucks to cut grass or sweep up around their shops. These entrepreneurs were full of unrequested advice about owning your own and doing-for-self. Yes, there was poverty and crime, but poor kids had daily examples of self-sufficiency and community pride right outside their doors. Nowadays, for many, the only examples they have of "black success" are people on TV or neighborhood hoodlums pushing dope. Most only see materialistic piranhas living lives of luxury amplified and legitimized by movies, hip-hop and reality TV shows.

In this current political and social climate of hatred and stale, stubborn racial division, we can't wait for politicians, the government, public schools or the criminal justice system to suddenly rectify itself and do right by its most vulnerable and persecuted populace.

Up to this point, we've explored the problems and some alternative initiatives specifically designed to address stereotyping, trauma, poverty, homelessness and other maladies that disproportionately impact poor children of color. Next, I want to explore the possibilities inherent with an agenda that empowers young people mentally, spiritually and economically.

***

"So, Mr. Brown, how much do you think it would cost me to buy that lot?"

I was driving The Dread Brothers home after class one day. At the time, they were staying in Walnut Park, one of the poorest and deadliest neighborhoods in North St. Louis.

Antonio, the middle brother, asked about a vacant lot we'd just passed.

"I don't know, anywhere from $500-to-$1,000," I answered, adding, "Or, you can probably just lease it from the city for like $5 a year."

"OK, OK," Antonio responded, but he wasn't finished. "So, let's say I was able to get two lots for $1,000. I could build a home on one of them and make money with the other, right?" I could see the cogs spinning in his natty head. He was trying to figure out the upside of owning land and growing food in his troubled neighborhood. "So, I can have a lot which makes money and my own home for less than $500 a month. Man, that's cheaper than renting!"

"So, let's say I was able to get two lots for $1,000. I could build a home on one of them and make money with the other, right?"
—SPP Student, Antonio

This was but one conversation I've had with my students that indicate they get it. Their enthusiasm about owning land, property and reclaiming poor parts of St. Louis inspires and concerns me at the same time. The inspirational part is clear, but I sometimes worry that I'm selling young people a fantasy, a pipe dream. Yes, I've gotten students jazzed about ownership possibilities but it's going to take a whole litany of players—political, financial and religious—and "buy-in" from the community at large to really make this holistic change. Our youth are ready, but I question the readiness of black adult leaders in adopting or implementing such a vision.

Let me provide a quick story that underscores my concern.

In 2010, I found myself mingling with some of the top black thinkers in America. The *St. Louis Post-Dispatch* and I had parted ways and I was working as a contributor and researcher with SmileyBooks, owned by TV commentator Tavis Smiley. Barack Obama was into his second year as president. Smiley and the Rev. Al Sharpton had embarked on a bitter public battle revolving around the issue of Obama creating and promoting a "black agenda" ...or not.

This conversation took on a more public focus during a summit organized by Smiley in Chicago. Guest panelists included Dr. Cornel West; Minister Louis Farrakhan; economist Julianne Malveaux; Rev. Jessie Jackson Sr.; Angela Glover Blackwell, director of PolicyLink; scholars and writers Ron Walters, Michael Eric Dyson and Tom Burrell (whom I had helped on his newly published book,

Brainwashed: Challenging the Myth of Black Inferiority).

I wrote about this at the time on my blog. More time was spent by this intellectual group calling for an Obama-led black agenda than was dedicated to them defining and implementing one of their own. This was unfortunate considering the influence and huge following these individuals possess. Some had been talking about a "black agenda" for more than 30 years. I couldn't understand why they felt the need to bash Obama for not uttering the words instead of creating and delivering it to the Obama Administration, then promoting it among their legions of followers.

The impotence of the black leaders that day scarred me. It was part of the reason, two years later, that I started the Sweet Potato Project. I felt a need to do something in line with Obama's federal programs such as the Healthy Food Financing initiative. Also, I was searching for something that fulfilled my personal desire to see self-sufficient black neighborhoods.

Make no mistake about it, industry may have fled metropolitan areas, but there's one reliable, vibrant, needed, yet unexplored area for serious community-wide wealth-building: land ownership and collective food growing and production. After all, everybody eats. Why not build food systems geared toward creating jobs and small businesses and community revitalization?

After some seven years of operating SPP, I'm convinced we're on to something powerful. However, I also realize that what I imagine will never come to fruition until we, as a people, adopt an agenda that involves, engages and challenges our young people to step up, reclaim communities and become stewards of their own neighborhoods.

To make this a reality, we must go back to move forward.

"Revolution is based on land. Land is the basis of all independence. Land is the basis of freedom, justice, and equality." —Malcolm X, 1963

When Malcolm X addressed the necessity of land-ownership, he was simply echoing a call articulated by other black leaders since the demise of slavery. In fact, as the Civil War was coming to an end, a group of black ministers were instrumental in crafting and implementing what became known as the 40 Acres and a Mule doctrine.

What Dr. Henry Louis Gates described as the "first systematic attempt to provide a form of reparations," was the result of meetings initiated by Union General William T. Sherman, Secretary of War Edwin M. Stanton and 20 black religious leaders from Savannah, Ga.

"For the first time in the history of this nation," read a Feb. 13, 1865, New York Daily Tribune editorial, "the representatives of the government had gone to these poor, debased people to ask them what they wanted for themselves."

When asked, the chosen leader of the group of mostly Baptist and Methodist ministers, Rev. Garrison Frazier, answered Sherman and Stanton's question resolutely: "The way we can best take care of ourselves is to have land, and turn it and till it by our own labor ... and we can soon maintain ourselves and have something to spare ... We want to be placed on land until we are able to buy it and make it our own."

Although the "mule" part of the proclamation wasn't added until later, Sherman's "Special Field Order No. 15," the land redistribution plan, was officially adopted by President Abraham Lincoln on Jan.

16, 1865. By June of that year, some 40,000 freed blacks had settled on 400,000 acres of land. Unfortunately, Lincoln's successor Andrew Johnson, a staunch southern sympathizer, overturned Sherman's order and the land along the South Carolina, Georgia and Florida coasts was returned to the original owners, aka white southerners.

Still, the mandate for land-ownership remained a priority among prominent black leaders such as Marcus Garvey, founder of the Universal Negro Improvement Association (U.N.I.A.); Scholar WEB Dubois; Elijah Muhammad, founder of the Nation of Islam (NOI) and many others. They all believed that land ownership and entrepreneurism were critical components to community development and the overall self-reliance of their race.

Even Dr. Martin Luther King, Jr. knew the importance of land as a valuable tool for self-sufficiency. While promoting his Poor People's campaign in the deep South in 1968, King charged the United States with parceling out "free" land to whites while ignoring blacks: "At the very same time that America refused to give the Negro any land, through an act of Congress, our government was giving away millions of acres of land in the West and the Midwest, which meant that it was willing to undergird its white peasants from Europe with an economic floor."

In his book *I May Not Get There with You: The True Martin Luther King, Jr.*, Michael Eric Dyson noted how King prophetically linked "white privilege and governmental support directly to black suffering," and thus, he wrote, underscored "the hypocrisy of whites who have been demanding that blacks thrive through self-help."

Two years before King launched the Poor People's Campaign in 1967, he promoted legislation that would put the onus of control in the hands of African Americans. In an interview with *Playboy Magazine* in

1965, King outlined a preferential $50 billion-dollar federal program that would specifically benefit "the Negro and the disadvantaged of *all* races."

"Two years before King launched the Poor People's Campaign in 1967, he promoted legislation that would put the onus of control in the hands of African Americans."

King's proposal included a massive public works project, investment in disadvantaged areas, job training efforts and subsidies to spur reasonable home and small business lending. Likening the plan to the G.I. Bill of Rights, King argued that the policy-based initiative, over 10 years, would lead to "a spectacular decline in school dropouts, family breakups, crime rates, illegitimacy, swollen relief rolls, rioting and other social evils."

***

More than 50 years ago, Dr. King predicted that empowering poor people would be the much-needed remedy to many of the ills our children face today such as poverty, hunger, homelessness, crime and "other social evils." That directive still has merit today.

The government's land-reallocation plan may have failed some 150 years ago, but it's worth revisiting on a national level. Educational institutions, religious and political leaders and wealthy benefactors should boldly revisit the mandates of Garvey, Muhammad, King, Malcolm X and others. Adopting a self-sufficiency agenda doesn't necessarily have to happen on a federal level. In outlining her "Plan to

Reduce Vacant Lots and Buildings," Mayor Lyda Krewson noted that the City of St. Louis sits on 13,200 privately-owned vacant properties, nearly 11,500 city-owned parcels with 3,400 vacant buildings, and 8,100 vacant lots. The mayor's data-heavy site provides valuable government resources, current programs and ideas for vacant property and land reutilization. However, it begs for a revolutionary, people-oriented agenda aimed at using land to empower at-risk youth and low-income residents.

As of this writing, Ald. John C. Muhammad's "$1 Housing Program" had passed the Board of Aldermen's Public Safety Committee. With full passage, the bill is a perfect complement to the Mayor's plan to reduce vacant properties. However, without a serious plan that engages low-income people and provides funding to rehab properties or revitalize land for food growth, the bill could wind up being another boon for wealthy developers itching to capitalize off cheap land.

Harkening back to the previous chapter, I'd be thrilled if rappers adopted and funded a land-ownership plan for the cities they come from. Imagine the symbolic power of a national movement of self-sufficiency and wealth-building spearheaded by rap icons. This would have a phenomenal mental, spiritual and economic impact on their legions of young fans.

At the Sweet Potato Project, we attempt to get students excited about the possibilities of entrepreneurism and purchasing cheap, available vacant land to grow and sell fresh food. My personal goal is to make this more of a reality than a whim of a naïve dreamer. The young people I have mentored, interviewed and watched over the years have convinced me that they are up to a bold community challenge. What if we answered their call for equity with a plan and with necessary resources to implement their own vision of self-reliance?

In the conclusion of this book, I will paint a more vivid and detailed picture of a movement girded by fearless leadership, government resources and community-wide support, all aimed at empowering vested millennials and low-income individuals to accrue and build wealth while taking ownership of long-ignored, long-suffering neighborhoods.

CONCLUSION

Let's Give Them What They Want

"Leaders are made, they are not born. They are made by hard effort, which is the price which all of us must pay to achieve any goal that is worthwhile."

— Vince Lombardi

Photo Courtesy of the Sweet Potato Project

When it comes to protests led by or involving young people, disapproving adults often ask: "well, what do they want?" The young people of the March for Our Lives or the Black Lives Matter movements, and even those who support "taking the knee" during football games have all been crystal clear about immediate redress. "Legislate gun laws that will deter mass shootings," or "Stop police from shooting unarmed black people" are but two clear demands.

Yet, distractors ignore their requests and instead make up their own defensible reasons as to why young people protest. Young gun control activists are "crisis actors," BLM youth are "terrorists," and those kneeling during the Pledge of Allegiance are flat out "unpatriotic." If we really listened and responded to our youth, perhaps there'd be fewer mass shootings, fewer people of color destined for prison at early ages or maybe more cops held unaccountable for taking innocent, unarmed lives.

Hopefully, at this point, you agree with me that listening is the first step to building future engaged, activated stewards of our communities, cities and country. However, another critical step in this leadership process is not only listening but challenging them as well. Other than voting, I've seen very little direct direction from academics, preachers or politicians as to what young people themselves can do now to address the things that cause them anxiety and angst.

Let's look at a list of demands that 60 organizations associated with the Black Lives Matter movement compiled in 2016. The agenda items included ending "the war on black people," political power, reparations for racial crimes, economic justice and community control.

Admittedly, most of the items listed are out of young people's hands. We adults must get our collective houses in order to stimulate effective remedies. But, the onus of a couple of those items, specifically "economic and community control" should be placed on the shoulders of young people now, pronto, today. We should challenge future leaders to do more than just articulate things they expect adults to fix. They should be compelled to detail what that "fix" really is, what it looks like and, most important, what they are going to do. We should have them outline the possibilities if they had complete political, religious, economic and community support. In short, how about we challenge them to make the worlds they envision a reality.

My city, St. Louis, is like Chicago, Detroit, Oakland, Memphis or any other city with disproportionately high crime, murder and poverty rates. I have spent decades writing, researching and exploring the socio/economic factors that lead to or fuel crime in especially poor, black neighborhoods. After all these years, I've come to one simple conclusion: We must empower people, especially young people, to make and sustain the change we all desire.

To date, the turn-to solution to crime and violence has been increased police force and mass incarceration. In April of 2018, *Patrick Sharkey, professor and chair of sociology at New York University and author of Uneasy Peace: The Great Crime Decline, the Renewal of City Life, and the Next War on Violence, wrote an excellent Los Angeles Times article that underscores how* community investment, not punishment, is key to reducing violence.

Sharkey details how "police forces have grown larger and more militant, prosecutors have become more aggressive, and criminal justice policies have become increasingly harsher." He explores how the punishment model that emerged in the late 1960s, "expanded and intensified in the 1990s."

"It's a system that's become increasingly militarized after the police shooting of Michael Brown in 2014, he adds.

These politically expedient, lazy reactions simply guarantee that young, poor people of color will be incarcerated most of their lives. Prisons, especially those in the private sector, will continue making billions from cheap, slave-like labor and communities of color will remain stagnant bastions of replicated poverty, crime and hopelessness.

To truly reform our criminal justice system, Sharkey suggests we move away from the "punishment" mind-set and turn to a new model based on "sufficient evidence" for countering violence. The community investment model, the professor wrote, is based on data that illustrates how community organizations play key roles in bringing crime rates down. In fact, his research found that "in a typical city with 100,000 residents, every ten additional organizations formed to address violence and build stronger communities led to a 9% drop in the murder rate."

We've already discussed the toxic environments adults naively (or stubbornly) expect young people to grapple with everyday unscathed. Like super-humans, we expect them to overcome the trauma of neighborhood violence and gut-wrenching poverty. They are supposed to heroically absorb the humiliating, daily wounds of stereotyping, race-based school suspensions, biased teachers and overly anxious police ready to shoot them, beat them or lock them up.

Here, I am calling for an ambitious societal reset; a new, revolutionary route based on community investment that sparks holistic, long-term change in neighborhoods and young lives under siege. How about we put our youth in control of their own destinies? What if we tried, really tried to listen and respond affirmatively? What if we imagined a different future? How about we seriously explore the possibilities of really giving our youth what they say they want.

***

As in Chapter Eight, I once again turn to a Hip-hop artist who's using his name, skills, fame and money to set powerful examples of replicable leadership. St. Louis born, Senegalese, multi-platinum rap artist and philanthropist Akon has raised the bar in the arena of innovative economic remedies for people of color. In June of 2018, the rapper unveiled plans to build the world's first "crypto-based city" in

Senegal, West Africa. The city of the future will be built on a 2,000-acre land gifted to the artist by Senegal's President Macky Sall. The city will operate on a new digital cash currency system called the "AKoin Ecosystem."

"I am calling for an ambitious societal reset; a new, revolutionary route based on community investment that sparks holistic, long-term change in neighborhoods and young lives under siege. How about we put our youth in control of their own destinies?"

Akon explained the new system thusly: "I think that blockchain and crypto could be the savior for Africa in many ways because it brings the power back to the people and brings the security back into the currency system and also allows the people to utilize it in ways where they can advance themselves and not allow government to do those things that are keeping them down."

This isn't the first highly publicized philanthropic endeavor of Akon's. In 2014, he founded Akon Lighting Africa with his entrepreneurial partners Thione Niang and Samba Bathily to provide solar power throughout 18 countries in Africa. Since its beginning, the project has produced 100,000 solar street lamps with a goal providing some 600 million Africans and African villages with jobs and access to clean and affordable sources of electricity.

Akon is one of those hip-hop artists that parents, churches and nonprofit organization leaders should be discussing and sharing with our youth. Highlighting his entrepreneurial endeavors is one way to generate progressive conversations that go well beyond the frivolities and fantasies that dominate the entertainment industry. We should be challenging future leaders to emulate Akon's example on some level. They may never build an entire city or electrify a continent, but we can encourage them to think about innovative, self-sustaining ways to improve and control their communities and guarantee their own economic futures and other's.

***

New York University's Professor Sharkey's research into the benefits of investment in community organizations to reduce crime is a wonderful idea. However, it goes against the grain of those who still cling to the antiquated notion that more police and tougher sentencing is the only viable solution. If the quest to give young, low-income people the power to reclaim their own communities is urgent, we must seek remedies from within those communities.

Lynn Da, founder of Buy Black Economics (the largest digital black business info store in the world), stands out as another prime example in this arena. In 2016, Da launched "Buy the Block," an initiative aimed at gathering individuals and groups to share knowledge, pool funds, vote and invest in properties and manage their own investments. This basic but powerful idea connects like-minded investors, makes investing as a group easier and carries the extra bonus of empowering average individuals to collectively own their own neighborhoods.

Da spoke to these shared benefits when urging potential investors to become members of the unique BuyTheBlock.com "crowd-investing" portal:

"You get to invest and contribute positively towards the betterment of the lives of numerous people. You would be helping to keep the dream of 'shelter for all' a reality. You would have done something you and future generations would be proud of for years to come. You can beat your chest in years to come and say 'yes, I was here,' in addition to making money."

Beating our chests to celebrate communal victories of economic and social empowerment in disadvantaged communities should be a welcomed outcome. Yes, everyone—white, black, brown and "other"— should be concerned and engaged in actions aimed at erasing historical inequities. After all, stronger, safer, self-sufficient black communities can lead to a reduction in crime and fewer public dollars dumped into this country's prison industrial complex. Yes, it should be everyone's concern, but it's the responsibility of black people to lead in efforts that will save and protect their children. African Americans can ill-afford to sit back and wait on broken economic, educational and criminal justice systems to rectify itself. We must strategically create alternative, self-sustaining systems that address the age-old maladies outlined in this book and elsewhere.

The good news, as I've tried to note in this book, is that there are many worthwhile programs, ideas, strategies and movements percolating throughout America aimed at addressing the myriad of problems that specifically and disproportionately impact poor black and brown youth. The problem is that most operate in a vacuum or are underfunded or go unnoticed. What's missing is a nationwide agenda that every social agency, political and grassroots movement, black church, public school and adult can adopt and implement on a unified level.

***

In the winter of 2018, I sent out a letter asking adults to help me gather 15 entrepreneurial-minded young people between the ages of 19-to-25. The goal is to offer a 4-month course in land-ownership, small business development, neighborhood food growing and product development.

The first person I turned to for advice was Cheryl Walker, the financial literacy expert and Community Development director for Stifel Bank & Trust I introduced in Chapter eight. Walker connected me to people in the banking industry looking for innovative ways to lend money that will impact community growth and stability. As of this writing, I'm reaching out to those individuals, hoping to generate support and community-wide interest in grassroots community investment. Still, the outcome of this experimental program is to, at the very least, have 10 kids owning their own plots of vacant land in disadvantaged neighborhoods by the spring of 2019.

The timing couldn't be better. As of this writing, our mayor and several St. Louis aldermen had been publicly commenting about the urgent need to reduce the number of vacant properties held by the city. Thousands of parcels of abandoned buildings and vacant land have accumulated in long-ignored, heavily black-populated areas on the city's North side.

This is the point where we must rely on our imaginations. Again, harkening back to the research on community investment, I'd like to see not 10 but 100 young people owning vacant properties in specific areas of North St. Louis. I yearn for bold, visionary politicians to earmark some of the millions and millions of public funds and tax incentives gifted to already rich developers directed to millennials of color, so they can become first-time homeowners. Surely, we can find the funds to help them rehab abandoned properties or move into affordable housing in targeted neighborhoods. Imagine if funds were also allocated for these young land-owners to grow and sell food or open storefronts to sell art, t-shirts, music or whatever talent they've mastered. Now, because we invested in them, we will have young people who are truly and personally vested in the safety, upkeep and economic growth of their own neighborhoods for the long-term.

Let's imagine further. What if the entire region, major grocery stores, bakeries and restaurants intentionally bought fresh produce from these young, urban farmers? I envision a major food manufacturing plant and a Northside brand, like Del Monte, Keebler or Nestle packaging and distributing products grown and packaged in the black community. There should be billboard signs, literature and church fliers that rival the familiar smoking, drinking, lottery, alcohol and payday lending advertising that dominate black communities. With a highly publicized, strategic plan, we can create empowering environments where do-for-self community-based entrepreneurism makes drug dealing seem as foolish, deadly and impractical as it really is.

Keep in mind, everybody eats. With a food-based community system, the possibilities of safe, stable neighborhoods, more small businesses, trucking and distribution companies, restaurants, healthier convenience stores, coffee shops and other and food-related enterprises can fuel an economic engine in disadvantaged neighborhoods like North St. Louis.

If all this happens and more, if it's replicated beyond the boundaries of St. Louis and across the country, I have no doubt our young people will step up to the challenge. Although my focus is on children who share my hue and my childhood experiences, I imagine an emerging template for all young people in this country, no matter race or gender. I wholeheartedly believe they can put their unique stamp on areas of disruption and despair. They can instigate and implement something that inspires and engages their peers, siblings and elders.

"With a highly publicized, strategic plan, we can create empowering environments where do-for-self community-based entrepreneurism makes drug dealing seem as foolish, deadly and impractical as it really is."

As Better Family Life's president Malik Ahmed said in Chapter One, and as Ald. John C. Muhammad reinforced in my "Reflection," black folk need to unanimously adopt an agenda or a harmonious national platform that's based on a "higher" or "collective purpose." We must seek alternative, community-oriented ways to systematically address the social, educational, economic and criminal justice atrocities I note in this book and others I haven't.

The $64,000 questions are these: Can we stop allowing stereotypes and skin color to dictate our passions and actions? Can we adults put our selfish, decayed political and social biases aside for our kids? Can we shift our national priorities to include a commitment to giving our young all the opportunities and resources necessary to create their own economic system and control their own communities and destinies?

I will end as I began. All this and more are possibilities...When We Listen.

CHAPTER REFERENCES

CHAPTER ONE:

Why People Are Still Protesting in St. Louis

Ryan J. Reily / 09/19/2017 / Huffington Post / https://www.huffingtonpost.com/entry/jason-stockley-st-louis-protests_us_59c13330e4b0f22c4a8cb27e

Heroin Overdose Data:

Center for Disease Control (CDC): https://www.cdc.gov/drugoverdose/data/heroin.html

Black Boys Viewed as Older, Less Innocent Than Whites, Research Finds *Police likelier to use force against black children when officers 'dehumanize' blacks, study says March 6, 2014 / http://www.apa.org/news/press/releases/2014/03/black-boys-older.aspx*

JEFFREY BROWN at TED 2015

How We Cut Youth Violence in Boston by 79 Percent

https://www.ted.com/talks/jeffrey_brown_how_we_cut_youth_violence_in_boston_by_79_percent

Why the Myth of Meritocracy Hurts Kids of Color

Study finds that believing society is fair can lead disadvantaged adolescents to act out and engage in risky behavior. JUL 27, 2017 / The Atlantic / https://www.theatlantic.com/education/archive/2017/07/internalizing-the-myth-of-meritocracy/535035/

Study: Cops Tend to See Black Kids as Less Innocent Than White Kids

March 10, 2014/The Atlantic / https://www.theatlantic.com/national/archive/2014/03/cops-tend-to-see-black-kids-as-less-innocent-than-white-kids/383247/

Community asks youth for guidance

St. Louis American / De'Marja Patrick / Jan 6, 2011

http://www.stlamerican.com/news/local_news/community-asks-youth-for-guidance/article_f734cd00-1942-11e0-8ae3-001cc4c03286.html

CHAPTER TWO:

Rash of elementary school suspensions in St. Louis area are a pipeline to problems By Elisa Crouch St. Louis Post-Dispatch / Mar 22, 2015

http://www.stltoday.com/news/local/education/rash-of-elementary-school-suspensions-in-st-louis-area-are/article_5efb0738-fda9-5532-b48b-eaae17f5f659.html

Are schools still struggling with racism? Teachers more likely to label black students as troublemakers, study finds By Richard Gray / April 16, 2015 / Daily mail.com

http://www.dailymail.co.uk/sciencetech/article-3041665/Are-schools-struggling-racism-Teachers-likely-label-black-students-troublemakers-study-finds.html

Blacks: Education Issues

National Educational Association

http://www.nea.org/home/15215.htm

How Racial Bias Affects the Quality Of Black Students' Education

Casey Quinlan / Policy reporter at Think Progress / Jul 18, 2016

https://thinkprogress.org/how-racial-bias-affects-the-quality-of-black-students-education-642f4721fc84#.n0i9p4q3e

Too Important to Fail: Saving America's Boys

Copyright © 2011 by Tavis Smiley

https://www.amazon.com/Too-Important-Fail-Americas-Reports-ebook/dp/B005LVNLOA

The Prison Problem

by Elizabeth Gudrais / March/April 2013 / Harvard Magazine

https://harvardmagazine.com/2013/03/the-prison-problem

"Education Under Arrest"

TAVIS SMILEY REPORTS, **PBS Series/ March 2013**

https://www.huffingtonpost.com/tavis-smiley/education-under-arrest_b_2947602.html

CHAPTER THREE:
Howard Gardner and Multiple Intelligences
http://www.tecweb.org/styles/gardner.html

Prince EA.com / "Why School Sucks"
https://youtu.be/MDreKHwrA-k

CHAPTER FOUR:
School fights are more complex than any one photo
By Sylvester Brown Jr. / St. Louis Post-Dispatch / Thursday, Jan. 22, 2004

Poverty and Progress: The State of Being Poor in Missouri and New Threats Ahead
Coalition on Human Needs & Empower Missouri
https://www.chn.org/wp-content/uploads/2017/11/Poverty-and-Progress-in-Missouri.pdf

What are the current poverty and unemployment rates for Americans?
American Psychological Association (APA)
http://www.apa.org/pi/families/poverty.aspx

Who are homeless children and youth in America?
http://www.apa.org/pi/families/poverty.aspx
American Psychological Association (APA)

CHAPTER FIVE:
"T.I. stuns when asked why rappers 'glorify' violence but call out injustices" The Grio
/ Sept. 15, 2016 / http://thegrio.com/2016/09/15/t-i-stuns-when-asked-why-rappers-glorify-violence-but-call-out-injustices/

"The Hidden Trauma Plaguing American Kids" / by **Sam P.K. Collins** /Think Progress
https://thinkprogress.org/the-hidden-trauma-plaguing-american-kids-cdd47a93c1cb#.okswzwcwu

"The PTSD epidemic in our most violent neighborhoods" / by Michelle Chen / March 14, 2014 /
America.aljazeera / http://america.aljazeera.com/opinions/2014/3/ptsd-mental-healthgunviolencetrauma.html

CDC's Adverse Childhood Experiences study: https://www.cdc.gov/
violenceprevention/acestudy/about_ace.html

"Inner-City Oakland Youth Suffering From Post-Traumatic Stress Disorder." May 16, 2014: http://sanfrancisco.cbslocal.com/2014/05/16/hood-disease-inner-city-oakland-youth-suffering-from-post-traumatic-stress-disorder-ptsd-crime-violence-shooting-homicide-murder/

"Understanding the role of trauma and toxic stress in the lives of children in St. Louis" By Kelly Moffitt • Feb 23, 2017 / Stl Public radio: HTTP://NEWS. STLPUBLICRADIO.ORG/POST/UNDERSTANDING-ROLE-TRAUMA-AND-TOXIC-STRESS-LIVES-CHILDREN-ST-LOUIS#STREAM/0

"The Limitations of Teaching 'Grit' in the Classroom"/ The Atlantic / by Aisha Sultan / DEC. 2, 2015
https://www.theatlantic.com/education/archive/2015/12/when-grit-isnt-enough/418269/

Bronx School Embraces a New Tool in Counseling: Hip-Hop / By Winnie Hujan/ 19, 2016 ? New York Times:
https://www.nytimes.com/2016/01/20/nyregion/bronx-school-embraces-a-new-tool-in-counseling-hip-hop.html

Franks' HCR clears Senate, establishing 'Christopher Harris Day'
May 10, 2018 / The Missouri Times / Press Release
https://themissouritimes.com/50989/franks-hcr-clears-senate-establishing-christopher-harris-day/

CHAPTER SIX:

LeVar Burton: America has sold its soul to special interests, and the Parkland students know it Mar.23.2018 / NBC NEWS / THINK: https://www.nbcnews.com/think/opinion/america-has-sold-it-soul-special-interests-parkland-students-know-ncna859266

Right-Wing Media Uses Parkland Shooting as Conspiracy Fodder
By MICHAEL M. GRYNBAUM / FEB. 20, 2018 / New York Times
https://www.nytimes.com/2018/02/20/business/media/parkland-shooting-media-conspiracy.html

White House responds to petition to label Black Lives Matter a "terror" group

Reena Flores/ Jul 17, 2016 / CBS NEWS /

https://www.cbsnews.com/news/white-house-responds-to-petition-to-label-black-lives-matter-a-terror-group/

The Parkland kids keep checking their privilege

Saba Hamedy / CNN / March 25, 2018

https://www.cnn.com/2018/03/24/politics/march-for-our-lives-students-checking-privilege-trnd/index.html

Early Signs of a Youth Wave

Young-adult turnout surged by 188 percent in early voting compared with 2014.

By Julie Beckcaroline Kitchener / Nov. 6, 2018 / theatlantic,com

https://www.theatlantic.com/politics/archive/2018/11/youth-turnout-midterm-2018/575092/

High Young Voter Turnout Crucial to Blue Wave, Per Harvard Analysis

By Alexandra A. Chaidez / Nov. 8, 2018 / the Crimson.com

https://www.thecrimson.com/article/2018/11/8/iop-reacts-midterm-elections/

Australian Kids Just Staged a Climate Change Protest - Check Out Their Epic Signs

By Carly Cassella / Ded. 1, 2018/ ScienceAlert.com

https://www.sciencealert.com/australian-school-students-skip-class-to-protest-climate-change-and-check-out-how-awesome-they-were

They Were Trained for This Moment

Dahlia Lithwick / Feb 28, 2018 / Slate.com

https://slate.com/news-and-politics/2018/02/the-student-activists-of-marjory-stoneman-douglas-high-demonstrate-the-power-of-a-full-education.html

Should an urban school serving black and Hispanic students look like schools for affluent white kids?

Hechinger Report / by Emmanuel Felton / December 1, 2016

http://hechingerreport.org/should-an-urban-school-serving-black-and-hispanic-students-look-like-schools-for-affluent-white-kids/

Oliver North takes on the Stoneman Douglas kids

Daily KOS / May 13, 2018

https://www.dailykos.com/stories/2018/5/13/1763994/-Oliver-North-takes-on-the-Stoneman-Douglas-kids?detail=emaildkre

Ferguson artists blur boundaries between activism and art
City Scape / By ÁINE O›Connor / Aug. 7, 2015
HTTP://NEWS.STLPUBLICRADIO.ORG/POST/FERGUSON-ARTISTS-BLUR-BOUNDARIES-BETWEEN-ACTIVISM-AND-ART#STREAM/0

Protester-Turned-Politician Bruce Franks Jr. Overturns St. Louis Primary Result
By Brian Heffernan / October 20, 2016 / St. Louis magazine
https://www.stlmag.com/news/politics/being-frank/

CHAPTER SEVEN:
Hold youth accountable, but consider human development in doing so
By Paul Meunier / 11/30/2012 / WWW.Minnpost.com
https://www.minnpost.com/community-voices/2012/11/hold-youth-accountable-consider-human-development-doing-so/

Survey: 63% of 20-Somethings Want to Start a Business
by Minda Zetlin / www.Inc.com / Dec 17, 2013
https://www.inc.com/minda-zetlin/63-percent-of-20-somethings-want-to-own-a-business.html

How Big Is the Underground Economy in America?
By Matthew Johnston | March 29, 2016
https://www.investopedia.com/articles/markets/032916/how-big-underground-economy-america.asp

CHAPTER EIGHT:
Jay-Z's Pitch for Generational Wealth
Spencer Kornhaber / June 30, 2017 / The Atlantic
https://www.theatlantic.com/entertainment/archive/2017/06/jay-zs-pitch-for-generational-wealth/532383/

Three pieces of financial wisdom Jay-Z drops in '4:44'
Jonnelle Marte / July 5, 2017 / Washington Post /
https://www.washingtonpost.com/news/get-there/wp/2017/07/05/three-pieces-of-financial-wisdom-jay-z-drops-in-444/?utm_term=.50e65f887041

5 Rappers on Personal Finance
Grant Sabatier / Millennial Money Blog /
https://millennialmoney.com/rappers-personal-finance/

I Apologize Part 1 in LA (D-Black/Tracey Mann) https://youtu.be/Z_HDo88u_zw?list
=PLACyuilx6Nr1JEVVMVfVYxAKrv-JSTeVL

CHAPTER NINE:
Obama Administration Details Healthy Food Financing Initiative
US Department of Treasury
https://www.treasury.gov/press-center/press-releases/Pages/tg555.aspx

The Truth Behind '40 Acres and a Mule'
by Henry Louis Gates, Jr. | **Originally posted on** The Root
http://www.pbs.org/wnet/african-americans-many-rivers-to-cross/history/the-truth-behind-40-acres-and-a-mule/

I May Not Get There With You: The True Martin Luther King, Jr.
By Michael Eric Dyson /(C) 2000 Michael Eric Dyson All rights reserved. ISBN:
0-684-86776-1
https://archive.nytimes.com/www.nytimes.com/books/first/d/dyson-may.
html?referrer=justicewire

Reflections on the Great Chicago Gripe Fest
by Sylvester Brown, Jr. / March, 28, 2010 / sylvesterbrownjr.blogspot.com
http://sylvesterbrownjr.blogspot.com/2010/03/reflections-on-great-chicago-gripe-fest.
html

KING's 1965 Playboy Interview by Alex Haley
http://www.playboy.co.uk/article/16285/playboy-interview-martin-luther-king

A Plan to Reduce Vacant Lots and Buildings by Mayor Lyda Krewson
https://www.stlouis-mo.gov/government/departments/mayor/initiatives/vacancy.cfm

CONCLUSION:

Black Lives Matter groups list their demands

by Maria Biery / August 01, 2016 / Washington Examiner

https://www.washingtonexaminer.com/black-lives-matter-groups-list-their-demands

Black Lives Matter groups list their demands

by Maria Biery / August 01, 2016 / Washington Examiner

https://www.washingtonexaminer.com/black-lives-matter-groups-list-their-demands

Rapper Akon is Building the First Ever Black-Owned Futuristic City With Its Own Cryptocurrency Called Akoin / June 28, 2018/ Blackbusiness.org

https://www.blackbusiness.org/2018/06/akon-buildingblack-owned-futuristic-city-senegal-akoin-cryptocurrencyhtml?fbclid=IwAR1EWQwLM-qkzBZzgVma8-PpRz6JLvwWt5 Q2s7qSQjeGKboQIt4MU3DgsM

Community investment, not punishment, is key to reducing violence

Washington Post / by Patrick Sharkey / Jan 25, 2018

HTTP://WWW.LATIMES.COM/OPINION/OP-ED/LA-OE-SHARKEY-VIOLENCE-COMMUNITY-INVESTMENT-20180125-STORY.HTML

Program Shows Black Entrepreneurs how to "buy the block" — Making Real Investing Easier than Ever

Nov. 4, 2016 / Posted by Staff / BBNomics / Black Crowdfunding Site

https://bbnomics.com/program-shows-black-entrepreneurs-how-to-buy-the-block-making-real-investing-easier-than-ever/?+the+wealth%21

CREDITS & ACKNOWLEDGEMENTS

It would take many more pages to thank all the people who have contributed to my career as a writer or those who have supported my many endeavors throughout the years. Let me summarize by saying I am profoundly and humbly grateful to you all. However, I must take a moment to thank those for their contributions to this book and/or the Sweet Potato Project:

CHEF JEFF HENDERSON

CHEF/AUTHOR/ SPEAKER / TELEVISION HOST

Jeff Henderson inspires with his emotional journey of redemption from the streets to the stove, sharing real-life strategies to help you achieve your dreams, no matter your stage of life.

From humble beginnings in South Central Los Angeles, to life as an imprisoned drug dealer, and then as an award-winning celebrity chef and best-selling author, Jeff is a role model for anyone who needs the encouragement to reinvent their life.

The creator of Food Network's reality series, "The Chef Jeff Project," host of "Family Style with Chef Jeff," and the star of the TV series, "Flip My Food with Chef Jeff," he is also the best-selling author of two books.

Jeff is the author of four best-selling books: "Cooked," "Chef Jeff

Cooks," "Pass it Down Cookbook" and "If You Can See It You Can Be It"

From overcoming hardship to identifying one's personal talents, Jeff reveals his hard-knock yet transformative life lessons and the secrets to rising above and realizing your potential. His dynamic and engaging presentations help audiences discover their hidden business aptitudes, make life-changing decisions, and gain a new foothold on the ladder to success.

Condensed from https://www.chefjefflive.com/

***

TONY NEAL

Tony Neal is the President/CEO of Educational Equity Consultants and Executive Director of the Center for Educational Equity. He served as Director of Southern Illinois University East St. Louis Charter High School for 11 years. Tony also serves as an adjunct professor at Webster University, where he teaches in the Media Communications department. our lifetime. Additionally, Tony has been a valued advisor and contributor to the Sweet Potato Project.

Condensed from eec4justice.com

***

BOLANLE AMBONISYE

Bolanle Ambonisye (Bo Lahn Lay Ahm Bo Nees Yay) heads U&I-RISE, which fosters individual, family and community empowerment. She believes: 1) regardless of the level of dysfunction, people – individually and collectively - have the ability to solve their own problems, and 2) group problem-solving is the core of empowerment. Bolanle offers two closely-related program courses:

*"Tapping Our Parental Power" workshops. Information and tools to help create a home environment that supports children's academic and life success

*"U&I-RISE": Uncovers and combats hidden collective conditioning that obstructs and/or undermines our ability to work together to solve our own problems.

Bolanle is a mother of 5 and enjoys African dance, which she also teaches.

More info at: https://uandirise.com/

***

MUHAMMAD RAQIB / REAL MEN TALK

Muhammad Raqib is Lead Motivator/Lead Empowerment Mentor of Real Men Talk, which provides educational, motivational, and youth-related services to parents, school staff, and community youth programs. The purpose of the organization is to motivate and empower youth by positively affecting change in their lives and communities. Real Men Talk provides motivational "tough love" speaking engagements, inspirational workshops and empowerment mentoring for young people from the ages of 11-25. Its major focus is on Educational Empowerment, Self-Discipline, The Power of Self, Choice Management, Conflict Resolution, Character Development, Life Skills Enrichment, Social Skills Improvement, and Youth Leadership/ Developmental Trainings.

More info at: http://realmentalk100.wixsite.com/realmen

***

DAVID ROBERTS (AKA D-BLACK)

ACTOR/SPOKEN WORD POET

 David Roberts-AKA D-Black (in poetry & self-written works only) is a Bronx-native who has been writing and performing poetry for many years. He is the son of an African mother (Sierra Leone) but born and raised in African-American surroundings. With this background, as well as his love & passion for acting, D-BLACK has done his best to feed others with verbal food for thought. By blending his social/psychological awareness with his urban/Afrocentric flavor he tries his best to express issues that promote Black awareness and unity. David is also an accomplished actor, beginning in off-Broadway theatre.

He is a 3-time winner of the Manhattan Monologue Slam. David was featured in Season 5 of the hit show, "ORANGE IS THE NEW BLACK." He also starred in the films "OUT OF MY HAND, DARK SEED" and numerous television commercials. Additionally, he was also part of the off-Broadway sensation, "Layon Gray's BLACK ANGELS OVER TUSKEGEE." Thank you, David, for permission to use your spoken word piece "I Apologize."

More info at: https://www.davidrobertsdblack.com/

This book is dedicated to the students of the Sweet Potato Project (2012-2018)

Barry Goins
Keith Young
Darryeon Bishop
Dashia Martin
Michael Watson
Damonte Williams
Keon Williams
Marquitta Williams
Elesha Harris
Charles Hill
Ella Stewart
Derron Neal
Myke King
Brittney Taylor
Charnell Hurn
Mirramoni Buford
Jenea' Wallace
Raheim Ware
Paul Miller
Darion Woodson
Jason Fitzpatrick
JoNetta Muldrew
Keyundra Baker
Frederick Butcher
Zavier Menears
Martez Joseph
Nadia Epps
Andivar Allen
Travion Johnson
Alfreddie Randell
Sherrion Roddie
Daja Wells

Terrion (Terry) Roddie
Marrisa Queen
Diamond Davis
Tytianna Parrett
Bryce Allen-Long
Briana Bennett
Dominique Hill
Arthur Scott
Shantia Darling
Antonio Johnson
Michael Smith
Edie Adams
Tamera Slater
Ranesha Sutton
Nautica Jackson
Raymond Blanton
Tahirah Quinn
Tatanya Carpenter
Treveon Keith
Aaliyah Slater
Davarayon Banks
Gavin Chapman
Billy Blockette
Terrica Washington
Trinity Wheeler
LaQuita Shay Davis
Corshae' Carter
Jerry DaJon Upchurch
Cedric Deandre Wilson
Myles Reed
Camron Vaughn
Davon Hemphill

ABOUT THE AUTHOR

Sylvester Brown, Jr., is a former award-winning columnist for the St. Louis Post-Dispatch (2003-2009). Prior to that, Brown published *Take Five Magazine* (1987-2002). Under his leadership, Take Five won more than 25 journalism awards. After leaving the PD, Sylvester worked as a consultant, collaborator and researcher on several books published by SmileyBooks, founded by TV commentator Tavis Smiley (2009-2012).

Sylvester has been a guest on Fox network's the "O'Reilly Factor," Tavis Smiley's syndicated radio program and Al Frankan and Dr. Michael E. Dyson's radio shows. He was also featured in a July 2005 segment of ABC's "Nightline" focusing on a community forum he organized featuring comedian and philanthropist Dr. Bill Cosby.

In the summer of 2012, Sylvester founded the "Sweet Potato Project (SPP)," a year-round program aimed at teaching at-risk youth "do-for-self" entrepreneurial skills. Youth plant sweet potatoes on vacant lots and are charged with turning produce into marketable products.

In addition to operating SPP, Sylvester continues his role as a journalist, writer, blogger (http://sylvesterbrownjr.blogspot.com/), community activist and public speaker. He has spoken at several local and national political, social, educational and religious institutions including the annual United States Conference of Catholic Bishops in 2015. Harvard University's Graduate School of Design in 2014. He also conducted a TedX Gateway Arch presentation in 2014.

Sylvester has been the recipient of numerous journalism and community service awards including the Terry Hughes Writing Award (2005) from the St. Louis Newspaper Guild, the St. Louis Association of Black Journalist "Best Series" (2005) award for the Pruitt-Igoe Housing Development series, the 2007 & 2008 "Best Column" awards from the St. Louis Association of Black Journalists, Washington University's 2016 "Rosa L. Parks Memorial Award for Meritorious Service to the Community" and the 2016 "MLK Legacy Award for Outstanding Service" presented by Beloved Streets of America.

Sylvester is a product of the St. Louis Public School system. He attended Soldan High School and Forest Park and Florissant Valley Community Colleges. Sylvester is the father of four children and grandfather of two. He currently lives in the City of St. Louis.

ABOUT THE COVER

Sweet Potato project students: (Front row l-r) Shantia Darling, Tytianna Parrett, Ranesha Sutton, Tamera Slater, Keon Williams, Keyundra Baker, Antonio Johnson (Front row l-r) Travion Johnson, Darryeon Bishop, Michael Smith, Arthur Scott

To Donate to the Sweet Potato Project visit the our website:

http://sweetpotatoprojectstl.org/donate/

Made in the USA
Columbia, SC
19 April 2019